OCTOBER 2017

TO MARK —
YOU ARE A TH[...]
INTERESTING [...]
FOR YOUR HELP WITH THE FSU
AWARD !

Take the Shot

I HOPE YOU ENJOY THE
STORY & SETTING !

TOM EDWARDS

TOM EDWARDS
(AKA TED DREISINGER)

ISBN: 0692952861
ISBN-13: 9780692952863

DEDICATION

To Molly whose partnership over the decades has
made me a better man. For Sarah, who in the years
she spent in our presence brought unfettered love.

ACKNOWLEDGMENTS

To Tall Grass Co-op: Melinda Haynes, Alexis Powers, Bob Clayton, Larry Castriotta, and Tammy Atchley Their input, care and honest feedback helped move the story forward.

To Tanya Fulcher for her keen eye and capacity to keep the story fully in mind and context.

.

i

CHAPTER 1

Thursday, June 12th – Fairmont, West Virginia

The man dropped his keys in the parking lot, at the Falcon Center Gym on campus, where Tony Cole was working out. As he picked them up, he slipped a magnetic, electronic GPS tag under the rear wheel well of the late model Chevy SUV. Now it was only a matter of time.

Trained by the military, he had been successful in his profession for several years. His kind of work was specialized, requiring patience and discretion – he had both.

The man returned to his vehicle, turned on his phone's tracking software and followed Tony around town for the day. That evening he watched the car cross the river on Jefferson Street and turn right on Pleasant Valley Road. Less than two miles later, it headed up the drive into Morris Park.

The GPS map indicated this was a one-way, mile and a half loop around a reservoir and water treatment plant. The man pulled into the Valley Lounge parking lot at the bottom of the hill, turned his car around, shut off the engine and lights and waited.

The vehicle he was tracking made most of the loop and then stopped.

Ten minutes later a white Toyota Camry pulled into the park and up the hill. In the dusk, it looked like a woman driver.

He waited another twenty minutes. Neither vehicle had left the park. He got out of the car and made his way up the edge of the narrow single lane road along the tree line.

His target had stopped moving some 200 meters from the end of the circular drive. He walked slowly and deliberately. Within five minutes, he saw the SUV and Toyota in the small parking area beside an outdoor shelter.

By now it was dark, the orchestral sound of crickets and other mate hunting insects filled the thick humid mountain air.

This is good.

Good because his target was isolated and good because the background noise acted to mask his movement.

Staying on the road, he walked past the cars and then quietly made his way to the driver's side rear of the SUV. Both windows were open, and the occupants were in animated conversation.

"Look, Susan," the man said. "I get that I'm married to your sister, but I have feelings for you. I feel it, you feel it. It's you I want and…"

"Are you out of your mind?!" The woman hissed. "Okay, we flirt with each other…we always have, but you and me? As far as I'm concerned, it was a one night stand. A relationship is never going to happen. You know it, and I know it."

The killer took the Beretta from its holster and

silently crept toward the driver's side door.

The woman was furious.

"Nothing is ever going to go further between us – E-V-E-R!" she said emphatically.

"I should never have come up here," she said turning her head away and reaching for the door handle. "Christ Tony, if Ben ever found out about this…"

The man stood, pointed his weapon at Tony's head - 'Pop, Pop.'

"What the hell!" The woman exclaimed. She turned toward the sound as blood and tissue splashed across the side of her face.

Those were the last words Susan Miller ever spoke.

'Pop, Pop.'

The slugs caught her before she could turn far enough to see where the sound came from and then everything went black.

The shooter unscrewed the silencer, put it in his back pocket and slipped the pistol into the holster on his thigh. He then took the black Busse BossJack knife from its Sheath strapped below the holster. Reaching through the open window, he grabbed Tony's hair, pulled his head back and with a single, practiced stroke, slit his throat.

Taking a rag and small ziplock bag out of his pocket, he wiped the blade clean, slipped the knife back in its sheath and put the baggie in back in his pocket.

He pulled out his cell phone and snapped a flash picture of Tony Cole's dead body. He then moved to the wheel well. Reaching underneath, he removed the GPS tag he had placed there earlier in the day and slipped it in his pocket.

A Beretta can kick a shell nearly 15 feet. With a small tactical flashlight, he carefully policed concentric semicircles in two-foot sweeps, looking for the brass. By the second sweep, the killer found three shells, putting them into the baggie. He started a third sweep extending the search area when he caught headlights of a car coming up from the highway.

Shit!

The darkened figure dressed in combat fatigues took off his gloves and moved quickly into the woods, headed down the hill where he had parked his car. In the dark, he tripped and fell. He got up, kept moving and disappeared into the night. He didn't feel the GPS unit fall out of his pocket.

xxx

Two and a half hours later in Morgantown, Monongalia County Sheriff, Jim Trach, called Gus Cole to tell him of his son's death. There was no answer.

Thirty minutes before the sheriff made the call, Gus Cole heard a knock at his door. When he opened the door, a man was standing on his porch with a Beretta pointed at his chest.

"What?" Exclaimed Gus. "Who the hell are you? If you've come to rob me, take whatever you want."

"Please step back sir," the man with the gun said politely. "Nothing will happen if you remain quiet and calm."

He directed Gus to take him to the kitchen where he instructed him to sit at the table.

"What are you going to do?" Gus said, his voice breaking with fear.

"Nothing," the man said, gently patting Gus on the shoulder as he walked behind him. At the same moment, Gus felt a sting on his neck.

He jumped up; eyes wide open in horror staring at the man. He gasped for air, clutched his chest and then collapsed on the floor. Quickly, the intruder injected the twitching man a second time. He went still, eyes glazed and wide open. Potassium chloride is lethal at one hundred milliliters. Each syringe contained fifty, precisely the dose in the each of the man's two spring-loaded needles.

The killer rearranged the kitchen chair, picked Gus up, carried him to the living room and placed him on the recliner by the couch. The television was already on. Pulling the cell phone from his pocket, he snapped a picture of Gus's dead body. The coroner would say Gus Cole died of natural causes.

The man walked two blocks to his parked car, got in and drove north on the interstate toward Pittsburgh. Just past Waynesburg, the ex-Army Ranger, and contract killer for the Philadelphia mafia took the Ruff Creek exit and pulled off the road. Getting a backpack out of the backseat, he headed into the woods. Five minutes later he was back on the highway, dressed in khakis, a polo shirt, and lightweight blue jacket, the camouflage gear rolled up and tucked away.

Twenty-five minutes after that, he drove into a McDonald's empty parking lot, brought up both pictures on his phone, entered a number and hit send.

Somewhere in Philadelphia, a man's phone buzzed. He looked at the photos. He tapped in, *the contract is closed*, and hit send.

xxx

After a job, the killer reviewed his work. He always did this.

He watched Tony for two weeks before moving on him. Fairmont was small enough to make keeping an eye on his target easy, and just big enough that a stranger in the city could go unnoticed.

Before he knew about Tony, he located Gus Cole in Morgantown and began learning his routines. The man was a workaholic. Every day was the same. He took the same route to his office, worked long hours and at seven in the evening he was home, where he stayed in for the night. The killer saw the flicker of a television screen in the window of Gus's home every evening. At ten o'clock, the lights went out. Gus was done for the night.

The stranger didn't draw attention as he asked casual questions at different restaurants and businesses about Gus Cole. He was friendly and gathered intel without raising suspicions. It wasn't long before he learned Gus was a widower and had a son with a wandering eye, living in Fairmont. The man stayed at the Super 8 out by the airport, telling the clerk he was making day trips to Cheat Lake and up into the State Park. The stranger was just another guy doing what so many other outdoor visitors did, hiking mountain trails and taking pictures. He was neither notable nor memorable.

The killer was professional and a careful man. Never one to rush the work, he thought everything through before acting. While the old man went precisely according to plan, the son's hit had three unexpected wrinkles – the female collateral, brass he left behind, and somewhere on his way out of the park he lost the GPS tag, probably when he fell. While he was not a man given to introspection or self-doubt, this kind of thing was not supposed to happen. It bothered him.

After finishing the job, he took a circuitous route

home — a long-cultivated habit. He covered his trail, traveling from coast to coast. When he entered his modest two-story brick home on Maple Road in Chester, Pennsylvania, it had been a week since he had sent the text and photos closing the contract.

While the man had a small number of clients for his services, none of them knew who he was, where he lived or what he looked like. All his work came through an internet VPN from a forwarding text service. Payments were made to an off-shore account in the Bahamas.

There was one exception. His current employer had provided him with a few jobs since the military. They grew up and hunted together with their fathers. That man was now head of the Philadelphia, crime family. Because of what both men did for a living, each felt secure with the other.

In the end, it was a mistake.

CHAPTER 2

Thursday, June 12th – Morris Park, Fairmont

Sheriff John Cooper looked around the crime scene. It was nine o'clock at night, and his team led by Deputy Sheriff Clayton Anderson was nearly done. Taking his phone, he dialed the number. Alan Swihart, the Marion County Coroner, took the call.

"Alan, we just found a dead man and woman in a car up at the Reservoir," Cooper said. As per procedure, no names were given over the phone.

"It's a strange one. Both shot in the head, but the male also had his throat slit. After initial forensics are done, I'll release 'em."

An hour and a half later, Cooper entered the morgue with the gurneys. It was late, and Swihart looked like it had been a very long day. After the bodies were put on the tables and had been given a cursory review, the Sheriff said, "This is a mess, Alan. How long do you think they've been dead?"

Swihart slipped a core temperature probe through the side of Susan's abdominal wall, took a reading and did the same to Tony's body.

"Well, it takes rigor about three hours to fully set in. Judging that you could lie them flat on the stretcher and by their body temperatures, they've been dead somewhere between two and three hours. What do you make of them being shot twice in the head?" asked the Coroner.

"If I didn't know better, I'd say it was a professional killing."

"Susan Miller and Tony Cole, killed by a professional? Here? In Fairmont?"

"Yeah," said John, "I know. There is something bigger here."

"I should have preliminary findings in the next hour," said Alan.

"Thanks. Let me know if you find anything unusual." John headed out the door toward his deputy, Clayton Anderson.

"I don't want to say this Sheriff, but we both know Ben was special-forces in the Army and did those four tours with Hank Murdoch," Clayton said.

"I know," Cooper said. "It's hard to imagine he had anything to do with this, but it was the first thing I thought about, too. I'm going to head over to his place to see if I can get a feel for him. Tony Cole was the son of Gus Cole in Morgantown. Call Sheriff Trach up there and give him the details. It'll be better if it comes from him."

"Got it, boss," he said, reaching for his phone.

"And Clay," the Sheriff continued, "a couple more things. When you're done with the preliminary forensics, let me know. If there is anything to send to the FBI boys, we'll do it in the morning. And will you tell Mary Cole about the murders? Sorry for dumping that on you, but,–"

"I'll do it," Anderson said before Cooper could finish his thought.

Cooper got in his squad car and headed to the Miller place. On the way over, he decided he was going to tell Ben what he knew about the killings. He wanted to watch his reaction. The Sheriff had known Ben since they were kids. This was not a visit he wanted to make.

CHAPTER 3

Friday, June 13th – Fairmont, West Virginia

Cooper lived in Fairmont his whole life. His father Robert "Bobby" ran a local funeral home. Like his dad, John grew to be a big man. By the time he got to high school, he was six foot four and 230 pounds.

After college, he returned to Fairmont to help his dad in the business. John was only needed part-time, so he joined the Sheriff's department as a deputy.

Four years later, the sheriff retired. On a whim, John ran for office. He was well known, popular in the community, and came from a respected family. Cooper won by a landslide, became sheriff and inherited a loyal fifteen-member team of deputies.

Cooper pulled into the Miller's driveway at twelve-fifteen in the morning. Already dog-tired, he wasn't looking forward to this. Climbing the steps to the front porch, he knocked on the door.

"Ben, it's John Cooper," he called out. He waited a few moments and banged harder. "Ben!"

Ben opened the door in a tee-shirt and blue jeans. He looked like he was utterly out of it.

"John, what are you doing here?" he mumbled, surprised at the tired-looking man standing in front of him.

Cooper took a breath, looking his friend square in the face. "I've got some bad news, Ben. There's just no way to make it easy."

"What is it?"

"Susan is dead."

Ben stumbled across the porch, grabbed the railing for support and sat down on the steps, looking stunned. Cooper went down the steps and turned to look at his friend.

"What? What the hell are you talking about? She is out with Janet Moore and said she would be back around eleven."

"It's after midnight Ben. Susan wasn't with Janet, Ben. We found her with Tony Cole in his car at Morris Park a little over three hours ago."

Cooper looked away, the sticky night air wrapping him in beads of sweat. He hated this. It got so quiet, they could almost hear each other's hearts beating.

Ben took a breath and ran his fingers through his hair. "How did it happen, John?"

Cooper watched Ben closely. "We don't know the details yet. A couple of kids went up there to park and saw the car. They were afraid the people in Tony's car might know them. As they drove by, their headlights washed across Tony's car. They saw two people slumped over. It scared the hell out of them. They called us right away."

"What else John?"

"What do you want to know?" John asked.

"Everything. Every damn thing."

Cooper was quiet for a moment. "You know I'm

not supposed to give you any information. We don't have any forensics yet, but it looks like someone crept up on the driver's side and shot Tony through the open driver's side window."

He paused before continuing.

"He took two shots behind his left ear. Susan was hit twice in the forehead above her left eye. We searched around the perimeter of the car and didn't find anything, no shell casings, nothing. We'll know more about the scene in the morning, but to me, it looks like a professional killing."

Ben's put his head in his hands as though he was trying to come to grips with the news. He was silent for a few moments then asked, "Do you know what kind of weapon it was?"

Cooper watched Ben compartmentalize. *Susan and Tony are shot to death, and he's asking about the weapon.*

"We don't, but there wasn't much of the right side of Tony's face left and Susan," He paused again, looking around, not wanting to finish the sentence, "Well, it was good sized caliber." John sat down beside Ben as he talked.

"How close was the shooter?" pressed Ben.

"Close enough to burn the back of Tony's left ear. I don't think either of them knew anything. After the kill, Tony's throat was slit. It didn't seem necessary, almost as if it were making a statement. Alan Swihart has the bodies at the morgue."

Cooper and Ben sat staring into the night saying nothing. Gathering themselves. John knew it would take time for Ben to absorb this.

Ben broke the silence. "Thanks for coming personally, John. You're a good friend, and I appreciate that more than you know."

John grunted a quiet, "Yeah," and put his hand on Ben's shoulder.

"If there is anything I can do, let me know. You'll need to come to the morgue in the morning for positive identification. I'll talk to Dad if you would like me to."

Ben looked like he was lost in thought. "Thanks, man, I'll come by. Tell Bobby I'll call him sometime tomorrow."

John stepped down the stairs and headed to his car. "You going to be alright?" He asked, looking over his shoulder.

"Yeah, I'll be alright," Ben replied, nodding mechanically.

John got in the car to head home. While his heart fought his head, he had to accept that Ben was a suspect. Even though Ben appeared to be shocked at the killings, his first reaction was to ask about the murder details. This bothered Cooper. It had been a long night, and tomorrow was going to be worse.

xxx

After John left, Ben sat in the dark trying to gather himself. Slowly, a thought began to emerge from the recesses of his mind.

Christ, they might think I did this.

CHAPTER 4

Friday morning – Encinitas, California

The window was open to let the night sea air into the small bedroom in Encinitas. The salt filled freshness of ocean breezes helped to cleanse his soul and spirit.

Hank Murdoch was sound asleep when the phone began to vibrate on the side table by his bed.

Bzzzzz – bzzzzz – bzzzzz

He hated the ringtones that came with smartphones, so at night he put the phone on silence.

Bzzzzz – bzzzz – bzzzz the phone continued to hum as it slid on the hard surface of the night table beside his bed. The girl lying beside him didn't move.

He fumbled for the phone in the dark and knocked it to the floor. "Damn it," he mumbled, as he patted around with his hand trying to find it on the carpet.

He picked it up, glanced at the digital time display on the bright screen – three a.m. He pushed the answer button.

"Yeah," he said in a thick voice, trying to figure out whether he was awake or dreaming.

"Hank, I know it's early, but I'm in trouble, and I

don't know what to do," The urgent voice started right in, and it was familiar.

The girl stirred, "Who is it?" she said.

"It's nothing," he said. "Go back to sleep."

"Hang on, man," he said to the caller. He got up, pulled on a pair of shorts. He walked into the living room, closed the door to the bedroom and sat on his couch.

It had been 5 years, but there was little doubt who was on the other end of the line. "What's going on, Ben?" Hank said, "You sound like crap!"

"I don't know how this happened, but it's bad. I can't get my head together," he continued.

In the years Hank and Ben hunted their enemies as an Army search and kill sniper team, Hank had never heard Ben react this way.

"Whoa, slow down, man," Hank said, still trying to orient himself. "What are you talking about?"

"They're dead, Hank. They're both dead!"

"What? Who's dead?"

"Susan and Tony Cole!"

"Susan? You mean your wife, Susan?" Hank said, still trying to make sense of his friend's animated voice.

"Yes," Ben continued. "My wife, Susan."

Hank was now wide-awake. "Jesus Christ Ben! Susan? Tony Cole, what happened?"

CHAPTER 5

Hank got up from the couch and walked to his kitchen with the phone propped between his shoulder and ear. He dropped a coffee capsule into his coffee maker, slipped a cup under the nozzle and hit the brew switch. He stood in the kitchen and sipped the hot drink while Ben talked.

"Susan went out with one of her girlfriends for a drink, or that's what I thought. We argued about money before she left and I was pissed. I had a little more to drink than I should have and went to bed at nine o'clock. Just after midnight, John Cooper came by, and I was completely out of it. He said his deputies had gotten a call about a car with two bodies by the old reservoir at Morris Park. When they got there, it was Susan and Tony, both shot in the head."

"Wait, back up," Hank said, his brain trying to process the news. "Do you have any idea what they were doing at the Reservoir?"

"No, I don't, but knowing Susan and Tony, I'm sure it wasn't good. I mean, why would she tell me she was going out with her girlfriend?"

"Do you think they were having an affair?" Hank asked.

"To be honest, I don't know, but I have suspicions. Hell, she flirted with him all the time."

"Any more from John?" Hank asked.

"He said no weapon was found, but there was little doubt it was murder. He wasn't supposed to tell me, but Tony's throat was slit. He said it must have happened after the shooting because there wasn't that much blood."

"Jesus Ben, this sounds like a pro hit by someone who knew what they were doing."

Ben's voice got deadly serious, "I know, man, especially the throat cut. We did a lot of this when we were 'haji and t-man-hunting' in the war. What I'm saying is that it could look like I did this."

Hank had no idea what was going on, but Ben's history with Susan had been a problem from junior high school. He had to admit she was attractive but could see through her like a pane of newly cleaned glass.

"She is self-centered and the biggest damn flirt in town," *Hank had said. "I'm just saying, man, you don't need that kind* *of grief."*

"Take a deep breath, Ben," Hank said in a practiced calm voice. "We've gone through a lot of shit…we'll figure this out. I've got a couple of things to take care of here, but I'll get an early morning flight out tomorrow to Pittsburgh and be in Fairmont Saturday night."

"Thanks, brother," Ben said sounding much better. "See you when you get here."

They clicked off.

Hank returned to the couch and lay down for the rest of the night wondering what the hell was going on in Fairmont.

CHAPTER 6

Ben hung up the phone from his call to Hank. He hadn't thought about it being the middle of the night on the West Coast when he made the call. The sound of Hank's voice calmed him down. It had been that way in the war. Lying and waiting in their sniper nests, they developed communication that was quiet, relaxed and focused. When Hank acquired a target and Ben sighted it in, Hank would say,

"Slow your breath. I'm watching. There is nothing but the target, nothing."

Sniper communication is brief and telegraphed in simple, lethal language.

"Ready," Ben would say. Hank then repeated the mantra, "Take the shot."

Ben replayed memory tapes of some of their missions as he headed to the kitchen. He was still numb but had learned to compartmentalize things. His mind was on Susan, but his morning routine kicked in. He knew it would help for him to have a good breakfast in the safety of his home. After returning from the service and marrying Susan, he took the house that had been a place of terror when he was growing up, gutted the place, redesigned everything and made a home for the two of them. His father had been a raging alcoholic and beat Ben regularly when he was young. The only saving grace was that his house and property were adjacent to the Murdoch's. When he and Hank became friends, their home was a shelter from the storm. Peter and Mags opened their home for him to come any time he needed. Through the high school years, Ben practically lived at the Murdoch's. Ben's mother and two sisters had fled the rampages of his father when he was in junior high school, leaving him to fend for himself.

Tearing the place apart was cathartic. By the time Ben was done, the demons planted by his father lay in ruins.

Entering the kitchen, he put on the coffee pot and mindlessly began his cooking ritual - bacon, scrambled eggs, and whole-wheat toast were his early morning staples. Finished cooking, he made his way to the front porch. He set the food on an antique wooden table to the right of the front door by the steps where he and John Cooper had sat a few short hours ago. The sun had already come up behind the house. He had always loved this time of day. The emerging light pulled the soft grey curtain of dawn from across the valley. When done, it revealed the vibrant green leaves on the trees along the edges of the Monongahela River.

His mind continued to process the news that Susan was dead. While their relationship had been a challenge, the good times were enough for him to continue to try and make things work between them. As the morning sun kissed the valley in front of him, it brought the promise of the start to another new day. And yet, he was overwhelmed.

The next step. Just take the next step.

Unlike the break-of-dawn across the West Virginia hills, storm clouds began to form in Ben's mind. Sitting there gazing into the morning light, Susan Miller rose from the mists of his mind like the Lady of the Lake. In this case, there was no Excalibur's Sword, only ghostly memories of the woman he had loved for so many years.

xxx

Susan was a country girl with ambition to burn. She came from a family of five, a sister Mary and brother Ted. Fairmont was not for her. She'd told her sister and brother that from a child, she knew she was different, destined for something bigger. She knew when she could, she would leave this two-bit hick town.

Susan had poor eyes as a youngster and wore thick glasses, the kind that draws your attention to what is in front, not what is behind them. "Four eyes," they'd called her. Outspoken and smart, she worked hard and made good grades. The teasing had stiffened her resolve to someday get away from this place.

It was in the junior high school where Ben first noticed her. Unlike the other girls in the new school, she had a different look and feel about her. The first thing that caught his attention was the way she walked, or rather glided. Susan Gallagher moved so smoothly that it almost seemed like she wasn't touching the floor. She had a freckled face, with a slightly elevated chin, a voice that was commanding, and for a young girl an artistic flair. There was something special, different. The kind of thing you try hard to put your finger on but can't.

He made a point in the second week of school to catch her attention. "Hi, my name's Ben," he said.

"I know who you are," she said, looking directly into his eyes. There was a confidence, a sense of knowing in this budding teenager that completely unnerved him.

His heart skipped a beat. *I know who you are,* she had said.

He had planned everything he was going to say, but when she looked at him, his mouth went dry, and the bottom fell out of his stomach. He wasn't sure he could utter a word. He stumbled, trying to keep the conversation going, "Where are you from?"

"I live in Hallsville," she replied. "There's a bus, but Daddy works for the glass plant across the river and brings me, so I don't have to ride the bus with the rest of them."

She'd said that with contempt, but also with a little hurt.

Mouth still dry, his mind blank, he managed to say, "Maybe I'll see you around."

"Maybe you will."

He did see her again, and then more. By high school they were an item, and yet she was an enigma. Although they spent a lot of time together, he was never confident of her feelings for him. Even so, in his mind, she was the prize. And yet, when the time came, she did leave Fairmont and Ben behind.

"I got an art scholarship to university. I'll be leaving in August," she had said. There was no conversation about how much she would miss him, or how she wanted to keep in contact. It was like Susan was following a star on the horizon and nothing else mattered. It broke his heart.

xxx

The porch came back into focus. Drinking that cup

of coffee, Ben wondered how it had come to this. His best friend was gone, somewhere on the 'left coast,' and until last night, he was married to a woman he had loved from the first moment he laid eyes on her.

CHAPTER 7

Ben took his dishes to the kitchen, washed them and put everything away. Filling his cup a second time, he headed back to the porch, wondering how Susan managed such a strong hold on him. He was no saint. There were a number of girls between tours and on leave. The damned thing was, he compared every one of them to her. The image he created of her had burrowed itself so deeply in his mind, it defied rational thought. He hated that he could not let her go, even when she was gone.

Sitting on the porch in the morning always seemed to clear his head. This morning, it was anything but clear. He closed his eyes and caught the scent of her closeness. In moments of intimacy, Ben felt almost as though he was floating timelessly. Holding her, feeling her breath on his neck and the childlike whispers in his ear, were both sacred and primal. There was a fierceness about her – dangerous almost. Their sex defied description. It was engaged, forcefully primal and intimate at the same time. When they were done, he would linger, she would move on. She was like trying to hold on to the wind – there one moment then gone without a trace.

Yeah, she had owned him even now as he came to

grips with her death.

He lost track of her during the war years, but when he finished his military commitment and came home, he was surprised to find her living once again in Fairmont.

xxx

Susan Gallagher held contempt for Fairmont. She kept herself busy with schoolwork, chores around the farm, but mostly dreamt of escaping this place. Careful not to openly talk about it except with her brother and sister, from time to time she shared her thoughts with Ben, usually when she was upset or frustrated.

"I'm going to go to away to college and NEVER coming back," she's said many times.

It was the way she said, "away from here" almost as if *here* were a disease of the body and soul requiring the cleansing exorcism of geographical relocation.

From a child, she knew that she belonged somewhere else. She was smart and direct and did not often back down, a trait reflective of her Scottish heritage. Her attitude in school was of mild contempt for those around her. Classmates said she was arrogant and distant. She probably was.

There was a secret in the Gallagher's home unknown outside the family. Agnes, Susan's mother, was born Agnes Campbell, a descendant of the Duke of Argyle of County Nairn, Scotland, famous for battles with the English. The surname's original spelling had been Cambel, meaning crooked mouth, an apt description flowing through the family genes and blossoming in the proud and cruel tongue that she possessed.

She drove her children to excel – the undercurrent

of bitterness that had poisoned her soul leading her to constantly criticize them. Agnes cultivated the bitterness and defensiveness that grew in the children.

"Do you want to end up living in this God-forsaken place?" Agnes frequently asked.

To the girls, "If you don't do well in school, you will marry some good-looking Dago boy and be stuck here, while his good looks turn to sand – yours, too."

There were rules about where they could go, how late they could stay out, who they spent time with.

"If one of those boys gets you pregnant, he will leave you," her mother said many times.

"You get in a family way, just get on a bus and don't ever come back!"

The constant pressure from home and Susan's difficulty getting along with her class-mates drove her to Ben. He was patient and caring, and maybe she didn't feel the same way about him that he felt toward her, but he was there and she needed some positive reinforcement in her life.

xxx

Sitting there breathing in the sweet-scented air of the West Virginia hills, it was like Ben could almost reach out and touch Susan. His heart burned with a sense of unspoken loss. He let go, unable to get his breath as he sat on that porch and sobbed until there was nothing left but numbness. He was spent.

He wasn't sure how long he sat there, but when he got up and headed to the kitchen for a third cup of coffee, it had been over an hour.

Clarity came to Ben's mind, between the front porch and the kitchen counter. He was going to find out

28

who did this.

CHAPTER 8

At nine o'clock that morning, Ben made his second call of the morning.

"County Coroner's office, how may I help you," the receptionist said in a polite and professional way.

"Sandy, this is Ben Miller," he said in a monotone voice.

"Oh Ben, I am so sorry about Susan," Sandy Wilcox said in a soft and empathetic tone. She and Ben had gone to high school together.

"Thanks, Sandy. I told Sheriff Cooper I would come in this morning to identify Susan. Is there a better time for me to come?"

"Dr. Swihart worked past midnight with Susan and Tony Cole. He left a message that he would be coming late this morning. If you come at eleven o'clock, I am certain he will be here."

"I'll be there," Ben said and hit the red icon on his phone, disconnecting the call.

Just then his phone rang.

"Hi, Ben Miller," he said.

"Ben, its John. You asked about the weapon when I came by early this morning. I didn't know. My deputy

Clayton Anderson was up at the pavilion this morning working the scene. He found a shell casing. It was a nine millimeter." Cooper sounded worn out and subdued like the man hadn't slept any better than he had.

"Do you have any idea what kind of gun was used?" Ben asked as the rational side of his brain working.

The phone got quiet like Cooper was trying to decide how much more to say. Ben heard him sigh.

"Okay, I'm going to guess it was a Beretta, and further guess it was silenced."

"Beretta? Silenced?" Ben asked. He was both curious and bothered.

"The kids that saw the bodies said they didn't hear anything when they drove up the hill. Their windows were open, and it would have been hard to miss the shots."

"I'm not clear what you mean. Couldn't they have come much later?"

"We think they arrived on the scene close to the time of the shooting because of the brass we found. It looks like the killer policed up three of the four shells, but was spooked by the kid's car and took off. We have a feeling it was a Beretta because of the distance from the car where we found the single shell. That weapon kicks its casings pretty far. The one we found was fourteen feet from the driver's side window. That's about all I can tell you."

"Thanks, John," Ben said quietly.

"Ben, you been in to see Susan yet?"

"No. I just got off the phone with Sandy Wilcox at Alan's office. She said he would be in by eleven. I'm going to stop by then," Ben replied, feeling the ever-increasing gravity of this thing sinking into his soul.

"Okay man," Cooper said. "Maybe we can talk a

little in the next couple of days, you know after you have some time."

"Yeah, sure," Ben replied. "Give me a call when you're ready." He punched the disconnect button.

Ben stood quietly for a few moments then went to his bedroom closet. On a shelf above his shirts were some shoeboxes. He took down the top one, opened it and pulled out two small, prepaid flip phones in plastic wrapping. Tearing open one of the packages, he inserted the battery and activated it. When the phone came to life, he made a call.

"Yeah?" a voice said on the other end.

A few minutes later, Ben closed his phone and went to work.

CHAPTER 9

Ben headed to the barn and climbed to the loft. The sun was up, and by now the building was heating up. The loft was even warmer. Light beads of sweat formed on his forehead and dampened his armpits.

After separating from the military, he and Hank had purchased a cabinet to store survival gear. He opened the doors and looked inside taking a quick inventory. Everything he was going to need was there.

xxx

Sniper teams are issued their gear by the military. When military service ends, that equipment remains in the hands of Uncle Sam. After six years of service, his M24 sniper rifle had become as close to Ben as a second skin. *Mary Lynn*, as he called the weapon had served him well. Next to Hank, *she* had been the most reliable part of their team.

"Damn I loved that thing," Ben said when he and Hank neared their separation date. Hank felt the same way about his sighting scope. They referred to them collectively as 'the girls.'

When Ben left the Army, he purchased a stripped

down M24 rifle at a gun show in Pittsburgh. A friend of his, Dave *the Indian* Price, was a machinist for Dana Mining Company in Dents Run, near Morgantown. Price had been a Warrant Officer 5 master gunner in the military. He worked as a supervisor in the mines and had a small custom gunsmith business that kept him busy in his spare time. Ben took the rifle to him.

"Uncle Sam has been considering a re-barreling the M24 to allow it to take a 300 Winchester magnum round. It will be more accurate at a longer range than the standard 7.62mm round of the current model," the Indian told Ben. "I worked on a few prototypes before getting out. If you are interested, I could do one for you."

A month later, Ben had a custom-built weapon that was lighter and more accurate than Mary Lynn. He called the M24 *Mary Lynn two*. Other than a few outings at a long-rifle range and regular maintenance of the weapon, Ben had not used it much. After Hank moved away, Ben left everything they had stored. There hadn't been any reason to use any of it – until now!

xxx

Just before separating from the military Ben and Hank purchased a pair of G4 tactical backpacks and loaded them with the kinds of items they carried during the war. The list included electrical tape, radio, GPS, multi-tool, batteries, headlamp, knife sharpener, first aid kit, gloves, tactical knife, water bottles, scissors, twenty-five feet of #550 cord, camouflage face cream, and three day's worth of military ready to eat meals (MREs).

Ben removed the backpack, slipped it over his shoulder, and removed *Mary Lynn two*. Taking the pack and weapon back to the house he placed them in his bedroom closet.

He opened a small trunk at the end of the bed where he removed a set of camouflage fatigues. To this, he added a pair of jeans, two changes of underwear and socks. He put them in his pack.

When he was finished, Ben took a second shower, dressed and left on foot to the morgue to say goodbye to Susan.

CHAPTER 10

Fairmont regional medical center was on the southwest side of the university campus, less than a mile from Ben's house. He walked the short path through the woods to the edge of campus for the last good-bye to the love of his life.

Ben had never liked hospitals. As he entered the building, the sterile smell of disinfectant filled the air. The walls, the staff, everything about these places was off-putting to him. The woman volunteer at the hospital's front desk directed him to the elevator and told him to go to basement level two.

Sandy Wilcox looked up as Ben entered the morgue. "Dr. Swihart, Ben Miller, is here," she called through an intercom on her desk.

Swihart came through the door from the autopsy room dressed in light green surgical scrubs, dark green rubber clogs, and a white, full body apron.

He seemed uncomfortable in the presence of his friend, rocking back and forth as he spoke. "Ben, thank you for coming. I wish the circumstances were different." He walked over and shook his hand.

"Thanks, Alan, me, too."

Pointing to the door, he said, "Please come in."

The concrete floors were angled slightly toward a drain in the middle of the room. A bank of ten, numbered, stainless steel body lockers in two rows lined one wall. In the center of the room were two stainless steel tables, sloped from the head with a drain at the foot, to catch body fluids during autopsy procedures. Attached to the bottom of each table was a sink with a water nozzle dangling from the ceiling like a slender serpent waiting for its prey. Adding to the stark, clinical scene was the pungent smell of formalin mixed with the faint odor of body fluids and excrement.

"She's here," said Swihart, opening the stainless-steel door labeled number ten.

"I am so sorry Ben. This will not be pretty. She was shot in the forehead just over the corner of her left eye. Stand here on the left."

He pulled the steel bed on rollers a couple of feet out of the enclosure. The body was covered with a white sheet that Swihart pulled down from her head and folded just below her shoulders.

Ben had seen a lot of death and done a lot of killing during his years in the military, but he wasn't prepared for this. He gasped as he looked at the pale-skinned, unmoving woman lying on the slab. The entry wounds were clean, nothing more than a two, small dark red circles. He knew why Swihart had him stand to her left. The other side of her skull had been blown off by the exiting rounds.

"She looks so, so small," Ben murmured to himself, trying to compare what he saw with the energetic, driven woman Susan had been all the years he had known her.

"You can stay as long as you like," Swihart said,

putting a comforting hand on Ben's shoulder.

"Maybe just a few minutes," Ben said in a low voice as lifeless as the corpse lying on the metal table in front of him.

Thirty minutes later he was outside the hospital, heading home. There was no joy in this day for him, but he was glad he had decided to walk. The sun and the gentle breeze helped clear his head, as he retraced his steps across campus and to the short path through the woods to his home.

The rest of the day, he puttered around the house checking and double-checking the gear he had packed earlier in the day. He got several calls of condolences, the most meaningful from Hank's father, Peter Murdoch.

"Ben, is there anything Mags and I can do? Dinner tonight maybe?"

"Thanks, Peter," Ben said. "I need some time to process this."

"I understand," Peter replied. "we just wanted you to know we love you deeply and have you in our thoughts and prayers."

Ben sat on the porch thinking about what lay ahead. His heart could not have been heavier, but in the military, he had cultivated a specific set of skills and knew how to use them. He was determined to do just that.

As the sun set across the valley, dusk turned to darkness, matching his feeling that the world he had known had become as black as a densely-overgrown forest at midnight.

At 9:30, he headed to bed knowing tomorrow would be a long day. He knew it was a risk to disappear, but it was one he was willing to take. There was another reason Ben Miller was leaving. The war had done a lot of things to him. He had been in confined spaces both to hide and at times to interrogate. Nobody was going to put him in a confined space. Nobody was going to lock him in a cell.

He would be invisible. He was going to become a ghost.

CHAPTER 11

Saturday, June 14th

At three-thirty the next morning, Ben woke up. One of the skills he and Hank had learned overseas was to regulate their internal clocks. He could tell himself what time he needed to wake up, go to sleep and let his internal biorhythms go to work. It didn't matter how long he decided to rest, the wake-up call was automatic.

He got up, brewed some coffee, made a quick breakfast and took a shower.

Ben put on the pair of dark green tactical trousers with cargo pockets, a tee shirt, and a long-sleeve pullover he had set out the night before. Over this, he slipped on a multi-pocket vest and a reversible reflective nylon jacket. It was June, but the mountain mornings were always chilly.

He added binoculars, a hygiene kit to one of his backpack side pockets and strapped a Gore-Tex Bivy to its bottom. The last thing he put in his pocket was a small portable Uniden police scanner with GPS.

On his way out the door, he grabbed his Wiley-X sunglasses, a baseball cap, and the disposable phones. It was four fifteen.

Leaving his car, he walked up the driveway to Cleveland Avenue and started into town. In twenty-five minutes, he made it to top of Jackson Street and headed down Pennsylvania Avenue. Fifteen minutes after that, he was standing just outside Colasessano's Carry Out on State Route 19 where he stuck out his thumb. Ten minutes later headlights flashed against his jacket. An old deuce and a half truck pulled off the road and stopped. Ben trotted up to the cab and opened the passenger side door. It was five o'clock and just light enough to make out the colorless trees across the highway.

"Where you headed son," the grizzled gray-bearded driver said.

"Just up the road aways toward Dents Run" replied Ben. "My uncle lives up there near the old covered bridge. We're going to do a little hunting."

"Climb on in, boy," the man said.

"Where you going?" Ben asked casually making conversation after he got settled.

"I'm haulin' a load of used tires up north of Pittsburgh," the driver said.

"Some boys down around Clarksburg have a recycle tire place. I come down here once a month, fill up my truck bed and take 'em up there. You'd be damn surprised the kind of money you can make haulin' and resellin' them wored out tires! I try to get back into Pennsylvania before it gets too light. I don't want them West Virginia Smokies catchin' me. Down here, yer not supposed to be haulin' this stuff without a permit."

After twenty minutes the old fellow pulled to the side at Sugar Grove Road and dropped Ben off. He waved at the driver and headed toward the Dents Run Covered Bridge, a half-mile up the road. Instead, in a quarter of a mile, he came to Chaplin Road, turned right and walked the last four miles into Osage where the man he had called the day before was waiting for him. It was five-forty-five, and the countryside was beginning to take on muted earth-tone textures.

CHAPTER 12

In the morning predawn light, a figure got out of a blue Mustang convertible as Ben walked into the parking lot behind the small department store. It had been fifteen since forging their friendship. When Ben was home on leave, he always made it a point to get together with Dequan.

"What you got yoself into?" the man said as Ben approached his old friend. "What you dressed all jungle fo? You goin' huntin' or somethin'"? I can tell you ain't be playin' no ball this moanin'."

The familiarity of this big man's deep melodic voice in the fresh morning air brought a smile to Ben's face. The two shook hands chest bumped and hugged.

Dequan Terry had grown up in Osage. His father and father's father were coal miners. He was big and strong and got an athletic scholarship to West Virginia University – the first in his family to do so. He was also smart. After finishing with a Ph.D. in electrical engineering degree at Penn State, he returned to WVU to take an academic position.

In Dequan's professional world, he became one of the youngest men to become an associate dean of the school of engineering. He knew how to talk to his white colleagues, but never forsook the dialect or the culture that had been his heritage. When he returned to West Virginia University, he bought a small house near his parents. It is where he felt at home. He particularly enjoyed his interactions with Ben.

xxx

On his walk into Osage, memories of this man floated through Ben's mind.

As a youngster, Dequan was on the Morgantown High School basketball team the same years Ben played for Fairmont. Their sophomore year they were in summer league together. It wasn't easy, but they became friends. On the court, it was all business, but off the court they found an unexpected rhythm with each other.

It began in one of the early summer games when Ben drove to the basket and Dequan put him on the ground.

"What the hell was that!" Ben exclaimed as he got to his feet.

"What's the matter boy," Dequan said. "You playin' or you cryin'."

Ben went right after the other youngster. It took both coaches and half the teams to pull them apart. Over the next few weeks, both of them gave as good as they got. In time, as often happens when competitors play hard and don't give in, they developed a grudging respect.

At the end of the summer, there was a tournament at Elkins. Fifteen teams from around the state played in the round robin competition. Ben and Dequan's teams made it to the semi-finals. Ben's boys lost a hard-fought game to his friend. In the finals, a big forward from

Buckhannon, tripped Dequan as he dribbled into the lane. He went down hard. The player was taller and outweighed Dequan by twenty pounds. He had been elbowing and grabbing him during the entire game. As he started to get up, the bigger youngster said.

"You better stay down, boy, if you know what's good fo you."

Dequan got to his feet, and the boy hit him in the face and then started in. Starting was as far as he got. Ben had jumped off the bleachers, ran onto the court and tackled the kid. In seconds a free for all broke out.

In later years when they saw each other, Dequan would say, "Boy, yo was 'bout got whupped by that fella from Buckhannon. It's a good thing I was there to protect yo white ass."

"As I recall," Ben replied, "I think you were the one on the short end of that stick."

Dequan's recollection of that event always made them laugh out loud.

That first summer those young boys found a bond that remained strong over the years. Ben looked forward to seeing his friend as he walked into the parking lot that morning.

After a few minutes of chatter, Ben told Dequan what had happened to Susan and his brother-in-law, Tony Cole. He said it looked like a professional killing because it was so precise.

"So? What does that have to do with you?" Dequan said leaning again against the side of his car.

"When I came home on leave, I talked to you about the work Hank Murdoch and I did in the military."

"Yeah," Dequan said. "While you guys were killing folks, I was trying to get through differential equations."

Ben smiled at the irony and stark contrast of their

lives.

"We did a lot of killing, mostly long-range, but there were times when we took people out up close. The killings were professional, Dequan. Double shots to the head and the guy's throat cut."

"Jesus," Dequan said.

"There might be other suspects the cops might consider," Ben continued. "But I'm pretty sure I'm going to be high on the list for these murders because of my training and because my wife was with this man, at night, alone, parked in a car."

Standing beside Dequan's car, neither of the men said anything.

"I didn't do this, man," Ben said, breaking the silence. "But it could sure look like I did."

"Damn boy," said the black man slipping back into dialect and pushing away from the car. "You some dangerous son of a bitch. So, why you be comin' up in heah all dressed like dis?"

"When I called, I didn't tell you what I needed, and I appreciate you showed up. I need to get to Cheat Lake and up into the mountains. I'm going to disappear until I can figure this out."

Dequan said, "Not a problem man." Then the big man smiled, "You might be crazy for a white man, but I can't see you doing this. Get in the car and let's get going."

They headed through Morgantown to the Mileground, picked up Cheat Road and within forty-five minutes, Ben got out of the car at the Burger King, just across the Cheat Lake Bridge.

"Thanks," said Ben leaning through the window. "Nobody can know about this."

"I get it, there is no problem here," said Dequan

leaning toward the passenger window with one big hand on the wheel. He grinned, winked and said, "Plus you the onlyist white man I ever really liked. Why I be talkin' to them boys on the donut patrol?"

They both laughed out loud, shook hands, then Dequan turned his car around and headed home.

The sun was climbing the sky as Ben headed along Coopers Incline. Two hundred yards up the road he crossed under Interstate 68, picked up Kelly Run and disappeared into the Cooper's Rock State Forest.

CHAPTER 13

Friday morning - Encinitas, California

Lying on the couch, Hank thought about the last few years. In some ways, Ben's call had done more than wake him out of a sound sleep. It had awakened memories he had worked hard to bury in the vaults of his mind. Yet his friend's voice, like the hand of a seasoned master safecracker, opened rooms of thought, causing memories to tumble out as if their hiding places provided no protection.

xxx

When the Twin Towers were attacked on September 11th, it woke the country to the reality of the vulnerability of the homeland. Both of them had just begun their freshman year at University. Hank dropped out and enlisted. There had been no question in his mind.

Ben did the same. He was ready, too. While neither of them knew what war meant, the boys felt an urgency to defend the country. They entered the service under the buddy system, permitting them to do basic training and advanced military occupational specialty (MOS) training together.

Hank and Ben signed up for eight-year tours. They expected three or four years of active duty in the field and the rest of their time in the reserves. If they stayed in for eight, they would qualify for lifetime benefits. They might even make careers out of the service.

Basic training in the military is a rude awakening for most young men and women. Everything from open bay barracks, uniforms, physical exercise, personal hygiene and shaved heads is intended to strip away any individuality, and molding them into single-minded working units.

During their first formation, Hank whispered to Ben, "Man, we look like we came off an assembly line."

"Yeah," Ben whispered back, suppressing a chuckle. "I love that 'no hair' look!"

Hank and Ben loved boot camp. They had hunted together as youngsters, so were familiar with the weapons drills. They were in good physical shape when they came in, enjoying the physical training, bivouac. and uniformity of it all.

Hank was 6'4" and had grown into a lean, muscular two hundred and ten pounds. Even in his late teens, he favored his father so much that people sometimes found it unnerving. The light brown hair he coveted might have been taken by the military, but his mother's brown eyes belonged to him, and there was nothing Uncle Sam could do about them.

Ben stopped growing at 6'2". He had blond hair with penetrating blue eyes that often made people feel uncomfortable in serious conversations with him. He was wiry, one hundred and eighty-five pounds, with excellent hand-eye coordination and ability to focus that was uncanny.

After basic and advanced infantry training, the boys applied for Army Ranger School. Both scored high on the Armed Services Vocational Aptitude Battery (ASVAB), qualifying them for practically any technical training the military offered. They could have chosen technical and safe support positions, but this is NOT what they wanted. Their country had been attacked, and they wanted to fight. After passing the rigorous field tests, they got orders for the rangers and reported for duty at Fort Benning, Georgia.

Special forces training was more challenging than they expected. The entrance mental and physical tests were rigorous, but as it turned out these were just a 'ticket' to the dance – the *dance* being the training itself.

Young men have an image of the special-forces soldier – strong, of few words, always prepared and kick-ass tough. The reality is that most have no idea what it takes. Hank and Ben were no different. There were individual skills in tactics, survival, language, and culture. They were schooled in tracking, resistance, escape and evasion techniques. This wasn't Rambo training, but a deliberate physical and mental framework that would protect them in the field. Even though they were enthusiastic, the image and the reality collided like two freight trains that had missed the switch.

While neither of them appreciated it at the time, they were becoming part of an elite group of soldiers, learning skills intended to save them in a crisis as well as carry them through the rest of their lives. It taught them to think in different ways, look for alternatives, listen carefully, ask questions and never, never say no until every conceivable possibility had been exhausted.

From the beginning, Ben and Hank learned the value of practicing over and over until everything was automatic. The course at Fort Benning, was challenging, but eventually, their skills became second nature, and they enjoyed every minute of it. After Benning, it was sniper school and the war.

Toward the end of their fourth tour, Hank began to wonder what was he going to do when he got out? He and Ben had become professional killers. Operation after operation, they tracked and destroyed, and yet nothing seemed to change on the ground. When he thought about the future, he could find no clarity. Each time he was home on leave, he felt more distant and untethered. He had become a stranger in a strange land. He and Ben left the military after their fourth tour. By now they had been in six years. There would be a two year tail in the army reserves, and then they were done.

After separating Hank kicked around from place to place trying to find a foothold in life. He was smart but had always felt like an outsider. The military had not changed this feeling. If anything it made his sense of discomfort worse. Were it not for Ben, athletics in high school and the imposed structure of the military, he wasn't sure where he would be.

Hank's lack of direction was a sore spot and source of consternation for his father, Peter. Fathers want the best for their children and Peter was no exception. He encouraged his Hank to get into school and focus on a degree, but it wasn't for him. Hank just couldn't muster the interest.

Hank dropped out of school after a semester left and drifted west. *Dropped out* was being kind. His grades were so poor, his advisor suggested he do something else with his life.

A year later, living in San Diego, he used a couple of years of G.I. education benefits for a Criminal Justice Certificate at Miramar College, barely scraping through.

His military training had equipped him with most of what was required. It didn't take nor did he give much effort.

Hank opened a small detective agency in Oceanside, catering mostly to returning G.I.s unable to cope with civilian life or their families. Usually, it was following unfaithful husbands and wives. The work was not difficult, but not satisfying.

He got a small consulting job as a civilian contractor with the military police at Camp Pendleton. The MP commandant liked the idea of using an ex-military special forces man rather than the local police when possible. Hank helped hold the lid on things, keeping some criminal problems *in the family*. But there wasn't much money chasing down Jar Heads.

He took a part-time job teaching an early morning boot camp loosely based on his Army Ranger training. The classes were filled with wannabes that liked to tell their friends they were in a physical training program run by a real ex-Army Ranger. The classes didn't pay much either, but they were a distraction. There was also no shortage of women who found themselves attracted to this tall, muscular, insanely fit man. The girls he had access to weren't particularly stimulating, but they helped fill the time.

xxx

"Hey baby," the girl's voice broke into his thoughts. She came out of the bedroom wearing one of his boot camp tee shirts and nothing else. "What are you doing out here? Did I do something wrong? Who called you in the middle of the damn night?"

"No," he said. "You're fine, babe. It was just an old

friend."

"I'm going to shower up and get dressed. I've got to get to work," she said.

"K," he replied, getting up from the couch. Walking over to her, Hank gave her a quick kiss. He patted her rear end as she turned away, smiling as he watched her walk back into the bedroom.

In high school and a few times on leave, Hank had been with Mary Gallagher Susan's sister. It had been casual but good between them. He thought maybe someday they might get more serious. When she married Tony Cole, the door shut. Hearing of Tony's death aroused feelings in him.

Hank headed to the shower where the girl was just toweling off. He wrapped his arms around her and pulled her in.

"No, baby, you missed your chance," she said with a grin as she rubbed his back. "If I don't get dressed and out of here, I'm going to be late."

He watched the girl slip into her clothes and followed her to the front door when she left. He stood in his shorts letting the early morning air bathe his body.

Married Tony. Damn. Now Susan Miller and Tony Cole are dead. Murdered in cold blood.

Hank felt a pang of guilt.

Christ, that's not right. The guy is murdered, and the first thing I think about is his wife.

As he stared at the ocean, the call from Ben and the weight of the past few wandering years seemed to wake more than his mind and body.

Hank went to his computer on the kitchen table, made a flight reservation for Pittsburgh.

He had two boot camp classes to teach, and then he would go to the beach to think. There was a lot to think about.

As he walked out the door, he looked around and took a deep breath of the ocean air.

Jesus, I haven't done anything with my life. What the hell am I doing?

CHAPTER 14

The breeze on the beach in Carlsbad was brisk, and the sky brilliantly blue. It was a place where Hank retreated to find solace. He walked down the steps on the face of a small cliff and tucked into a shady spot among the large boulders on the sand. It was still early in the day, and the sun was climbing out of the east. Small ground squirrels chased one another in and out of spaces between the rocks. For a few moments, he listened to the sound of the surf and the chatter of the seagulls. Pelicans and Cormorants scanned the water as they glided by, inches above the surface. He closed his eyes, took a deep breath feeling the salt air cleanse his lungs and settled into a quiet daydream.

xxx

The instructors at Fort Benning noticed how well Hank and Ben worked together. There was a natural rhythm as they progressed through training. First Sergeant John Harrington, one of their instructors, brought it to the attention of Captain O'Connor. Harrington said he thought they had a unique connection. It was an indefinable resonance that he called *that thing.* Training can save a team's life, but this was something more. Jenkins listened and approached the young men.

"Specialists Murdoch and Miller, we have been watching you over the course of your ranger training," began O'Connor. "You boys have done well. After seeing your progress, we think the two of you might make a good team. We want to send you to sniper school when you are finished with us."

"What's that mean?" asked Hank, the thought exciting him.

"There would be a further seven weeks of training to enhance the tracking and assimilating skills you have been learning. You would, of course, be taught long-range target acquisition. In essence, you would become self-sufficient ghosts learning to penetrate and exit very unsafe real estate. Your job would be to identify and remove undesirable targets. Sniper teams are of varying sizes from two to six men. Larger teams have more firepower, but a bigger footprint to protect. Two-man teams are more vulnerable but more able to remain invisible."

"Can you tell us a little more about the training?" Ben asked.

"The course will enhance your skills in marksmanship, target detection and acquisition, range estimation, and stalking. If you pass, you will receive a diploma, an MOS of 11 Bravo, and go to work," O'Connor said.

The boys looked at each other and in unison said, "When can we start?"

"Let's get you done here first,' said O'Connor. "In the meantime, we'll do some of the preliminary paperwork to see if we can expedite this thing."

As soon as they completed Ranger training, they headed straight to sniper school. Their instructors saw the same thing Harrington and O'Connor had and put them into a two-man team. Hank and Ben could not have been more pleased.

While both young men were talented shooters, Ben was the better of the two. He would shoot. Hank would spot and identify the targets.

They graduated and took a thirty-day leave home before their first assignment. From the day they began basic training, apart from a few days for travel and a short leave before Ranger school, it had been eight months to their first classified mission in Iraq.

It was the first but was far from their last. The boys learned sniping is a lonely and patient craft. It required blending into the landscape and remaining quietly motionless, often for hours, sometimes days at a time, waiting for the opportunity to *take the shot*.

Ben was good. His natural ability along with the training he received made him consistently accurate up to 600 meters and, if necessary, 800 meters.

During their first two tours of duty, they successfully acquired all but one of their assigned targets and developed a reputation among their peers.

These boys had grown up together, played and argued together and were as much brothers as if they had both come from Margaret Murdoch's womb. They were a damn good team. There was little doubt they had *that thing*.

xxx

When Hank came out of his reverie, the sun had moved overhead and to the west, putting him in the early afternoon heat. He stood up, looked out at the ocean, sighed and headed back to his apartment.

Saturday morning, he was on his way home to West Virginia.

CHAPTER 15

Saturday, June 14th

Ben made his way into the forest two clicks northeast of the Overlook, between Clay Run and Cooper's Rock Road. He reconned the area and found a small gully where he set up camp. It didn't take long for him to pitch his camouflage Bivy tent. For all practical purposes, he was invisible. There would be no fires, and someone would have to walk right up to his position to have any idea he was there. Most people thought of Afghanistan as barren and rocky, but he and Hank had built nests in areas that reminded him of the West Virginia hills where he had grown up.

It had been several years since he had built a nest to conceal himself. He was surprised how quickly his training came back.

Hungry, he tucked into his tent and opened one of the MREs. It contained beef stew and rice with a flameless heater to warm them up. The pack also included crackers with a peanut butter spread, some candy, and dessert. While he was overseas, this was the way he ate. Now he was in the field again, and it brought back ghosts from the past.

He remembered one of their early assignments in Afghanistan. Their intel indicated couriers were carrying money on a certain mountain trail. Their task was to take one of them out, sending a message this route was too dangerous. Under Islamic tradition, money is not transferred through banks but operates under Hawala, a network of money brokers that move cash on an honor system. Large sums are carried by couriers. There are no records, no promissory notes – nothing. It just happens.

It was a cold late spring morning in the Koregal Valley of Kunar Province. Hank and Ben set their nest on a mountainside at the base of a large pine tree. A small dugout, and ground debris as a covering, they were invisible.

They waited a week before making a positive identification. Hank set the range. Ben took the shot. Five hundred ten meters and it was done. The courier never heard a sound.

After meeting the extraction team at their assigned rendezvous point, they rode in a small convoy of Humvees toward Kandahar. It was a two-stage withdrawal. They arrived at the second rendezvous coordinate for a helicopter pick up. As they pulled to a stop, there was an ambush. Everyone cleared out of their vehicles and ran for cover. Ben made it safely behind a boulder – Hank didn't.

"Christ, I'm hit!" Hank screamed. Impulsively, Ben leaped from behind his place of safety and under fire grabbed the strap of Hank's pack dragging him out of harm's way.

"Hang in there," cried Ben as Hank gasped for air.

The medic had a flesh wound in the leg, but he was able to crawl over to the boys.

"Cut his body armor off!" he shouted in the chaos.

The radioman called in coordinates for an air strike. There had been nine men in the three Hummers. Two besides Hank were wounded, and two were killed. For ten long minutes, they took and returned fire. Suddenly out of nowhere, tracer rounds came hurtling to the ground like the thunderbolts of Zeus. Then everything got deadly quiet. The C-130 gunship made a second pass, and as quickly as it had begun, it was over.

The radioman had kept in communication with their base during the entire firefight. The Medevac had been dispatched and was waiting outside the kill zone. As soon as it was cleared, it swooped into the site. In the time it took to suppress the enemy and the Medevac to come in for the wounded and dead, Hank had been field stabilized. The medics redressed his wound and the chopper headed for Bagram hospital. Hank lost consciousness.

On the flight in, Ben was terrified at the prospect of losing Hank. All he could do was pray and encourage his partner and friend. "Look at me, man, look at me! You are going to make it," he shouted, as the copter left the ground. "Goddammit, Murdoch, where the hell am I going to find another spotter! I need you, man. I need you!" He sat back and felt tears streaming down his face.

From Bagram, Hank was evacuated 4,200 miles to Germany where he was operated on.

Ben did not see him again for a month.

CHAPTER 16

Saturday, June 14th

The American Airlines flight from San Diego to Pittsburgh took nearly seven hours including a forty-five-minute layover in Chicago. Hank traveled light with one carry-on and a backpack. While he wasn't bringing much luggage, there was a lot of mental baggage that came alive on the nearly four-hour leg to Chicago. Almost as if he had been channeling Ben, his mind wandered to the day he was hit.

xxx

Those first few hazy days in the hospital, Hank remembered practically nothing after being shot at the rendezvous coordinates for their final leg to Kandahar. Things came slowly back.

The burning sensation from the round in the chest was a like a red-hot poker. Hank couldn't get his breath. He panicked as he gasped for air, but no matter how hard he tried to inhale, he could get none.

He remembered Ben pulling him across the ground, a medic shouting and covering his chest. He caught a breath, but the searing pain was almost unbearable. There was a sharp sting in his arm, and the next thing he remembered was being offloaded by a team of medics at Ramstein Air Base in Germany then flown to Regensburg hospital where surgery was performed. It all seemed to happen so fast. He had been unconscious since the evacuation, swimming in a sea of narcotic and antibiotics during the hours of transport.

xxx

Hank's mind snapped back to reality as the wheels of the Boeing 737 made a bumpy landing at the Chicago O'Hare International Airport.

Getting off the plane, he stretched his legs, had lunch and a cup of coffee before arriving at the new gate where he picked up the final leg of the flight.

The Pittsburgh flight was on a commuter. He had been lucky on the San Diego-to-Chicago leg to get an exit row. This time, his knees were in full contact with the back of the seat in front of him. Worse, his seatmate was a large man with hygiene issues. As he stepped off the plane in Pittsburgh and stretched his legs, he felt like he had been born again!

Walking along the brightly lit concourse with arched ceilings he made his way to the car rental. Ten minutes later he was heading south on Interstate 376, in a black Chevrolet convertible, its top down, toward Rosslyn Farms where he would pick up I-79 South.

He found an oldies station on the XM radio and cranked up the volume. He felt alive as the wind blew through his long brown hair. It wouldn't be long before he smelled that pure West Virginia mountain air.

Picking up his cell phone and made a call. "Ben, it's

63

me. I just picked up a car in Pittsburgh and headed in. My ETA is about an hour forty-five. Call me when you get this." He disconnected and settled in, Fairmont bound.

Damn! Being home will be good!

CHAPTER 17

As Hank hit the outskirts of Washington, PA, his mind wandered back to Germany again and the days and months following his return to the U.S.

xxx

The doctors at Regensburg kept him for four weeks after the operation to make sure the overseas Medevac flight had not caused any complications. He had just gotten orders for Walter Reed when Ben walked into his room. Hank was thrilled.

"Hey Bro," Ben said in an upbeat and cheery voice. "Damn, this place is like a resort compared to the way we've been living the past few years. You look good, man, a sight for sore eyes."

"So, what the hell happened?" Hank asked cranking the bed into a half sitting position. "I only have bits and pieces of memory that have come back. I do remember you could have gotten yourself killed."

"Yeah, well, I didn't, and here we are. Plus, I don't know what I would have done without your sorry ass," Ben replied with a grin.

"Seriously man, I owe you my life," Hank said, his

65

smile disappearing.

They weren't much different than most men, young or old. Expressing affection generally came in the form of verbal banter. Both knew how close it had been, and although they made light of it, their exchanges belied the deeply rich and unspoken bond they had with each other.

Hank told Ben he was going to be sent Stateside to Walter Reed, and then probably back to Fort Campbell. Ben said he knew and had gotten orders for Fort McNair near the hospital, on temporary duty until Hank was discharged.

From Regensburg, he was Medevac'd to Andrews Airforce Base and to Walter Reed. Over the next several weeks, before getting orders for Fort Campbell, and discharging from the hospital, Hank received comprehensive therapy. By time he left Walter Reed, he was nearly as fit as he had been before he was shot.

At Fort Campbell, he was put on temporary duty doing administrative work. Ben was also reassigned to Campbell and served in the pre-ranger program.

By now, with breaks between four tours he and Ben had served, they were nearly at the end of their six-year enlistment. Internal military recruiters tried to get them to re-enlist, but they had done enough and in the fall of 2009, the two men separated from the army and returned to Fairmont, in those *West By God Virginia Hills*.

CHAPTER 18

Passing through Morgantown, Hank called Ben again, once more getting voice mail. Twenty minutes later he pulled into the tree-shaded driveway of the home he had known for most of his life. His father and mother were standing in front of the house. Moments later, they were in each other's arms. Peter and Mags Murdoch, had not seen their son in nearly five years.

"Oh Hank, it's so good to have you home," Mags said, tears trickling down her cheeks.

"You look well, son," Peter said.

"Thanks, Dad, it's all that clean California living and ocean air," he replied with a broad smile.

"Let's get you in the house," his mother said. Once inside, she told him to put his things in his room and asked whether he was hungry.

"When I knew you were coming, I made your favorite," she said with a smile.

Hank's taste came instantly alive the moment he walked in the door – the familiar smell of roast beef, Yorkshire pudding and gravy filled the air. The family's background was English and this was their traditional meal. To Hank, there was nothing better. While he had become much less of a meat eater in California, this meal was the comfort food of all comfort foods.

She knew precisely what Hank needed. He returned and sat with his parents in the dining room. In less than ten minutes, it was as though he had never been away.

They got caught up with small talk, telling stories and enjoying each other's company.

"I've been trying to call Ben since leaving California," said Hank, with a little frustration in his voice.

"He's gone," Peter said.

"Gone?" Hank said his voice raising. "What do you mean gone?"

"We wanted to wait until you settled in, but this afternoon John Cooper came by asking whether we had seen him. We told him we hadn't. He was at Alan Swihart's late yesterday morning to identify Susan's body. After John came by, we called Alan. He said Ben had been there in the morning, stayed with Susan for thirty minutes and left," Mags added.

"Jim Wilkinson, one of my colleagues, saw him walking up Campus Drive past Duval-Rosier Field, sometime in the early afternoon. It looked like he was heading home," Peter said. "I talked to Ben late yesterday afternoon and invited him to dinner, but he said he needed some personal time. I told him we loved him, and the door was open twenty-four-seven and that we completely understood."

"Dad, I don't get it. Ben called me when he found out about Susan and knew I was coming. Where would he have gone? I want to go over and check out his place after dinner."

"I agree, it doesn't feel right. I'll come with you and we can take a look around."

When they finished eating, the two men walked

along the path through the woods connecting their two properties. They crossed the driveway and open gravel space where Ben's Honda sedan was parked.

They climbed the wooden steps, and crossed the porch to the front door.

"Ben, it's Hank," he said banging on the front door. Nothing. "His car is here, he must be around somewhere."

They walked back down the steps and followed the drive to the small barn that Ben and Susan used for storage. Entering the building, they looked around. Nothing seemed disturbed. There was a ladder leaning against the loft.

"Let me go up there and see if I can see anything."

In the loft, he saw the cabinet he and Ben had stored gear in when they separated from the Army.

"There's not much up here but some junk and an old metal cabinet. I'll take a quick look around."

Opening his smartphone, he unlocked a small security program where he kept passwords and other personal information. He searched for *Gear*, and the combination for the cabinet appeared on the screen. The padlock had a key slot and four number code. He and Ben had done this purposely in case for some reason the combination was lost.

He dialed the combination and opened the door.

Holy shit!

While Hank's things were still there, Ben's backpack, sniper rifle and other items were gone.

"Nothing here, Dad," said Hank as he quietly closed the cabinet doors and spun the lock. He would come back later and do a more careful inventory. "Let's recheck the house."

Walking back to the house, Hank's mind was racing.

What's going on? Where is he? What the hell is Ben thinking!

They walked around the house, peering in windows. Returning to the porch, Hank tried the door. It was open.

"Maybe we shouldn't go in," said Peter, looking uncomfortable.

"Don't worry about it, Dad. We'll just take a quick look around, but be sure not to touch anything," Hank said.

The front door opened into a rustic living room that was the width of the entire house. The walls were knotty pine, giving the interior a clean and faintly fresh odor.

Across the room and to the right was an earth tone granite island separating the kitchen from the living room. As they looked around, their eyes simultaneously saw an object lying on the island countertop. It was a cellphone...Ben's cell phone.

In Hank's mind there was little doubt Ben had gone to ground somewhere.

CHAPTER 19

Sunday, June 15th

Sunday, Hank spent time revisiting familiar places of his youth. He walked around the high school grounds, re-reading the words of wisdom chiseled in stone above the doors of the building's entrances. Next was the stadium where he, Ben and John Cooper had played football together. Sitting in the stands, the sounds of another day and time resonated in his mind – Friday nights, fresh mown grass, bright lights and locker-room sweat.

He went to the armory where so many basketball games had taken place. After that, he crossed the river to Morris Park where Susan and Tony had been murdered. He drove the loop and headed back across the river.

By the time Hank pulled into the First Baptist Church parking lot on Fairmont Avenue, it was late afternoon. The minister, Ed Arnott, and the church had been an important part of his family's life. He had planned to sit in the parking lot behind the church, figuring this was an out of the way place to sit and think.

Pastor Ed was in his office. Hank was surprised to

see him there on a Sunday afternoon. He knocked on the office window. "Hank Murdoch," the minister said opening the back door to the church with an outstretched hand and a warm smile. "What are you doing in town?"

"I came home because of the murders of Tony Cole and Ben Miller's wife Susan."

"Yes, yes. What a terrible thing. We were all devastated to learn the news." He said, the smile disappearing from his face. "I was just finishing up before heading home. I had a wedding after church today. I just called Fan to tell her I was on the way home. We're going to take a few days off this week. I wanted everything tidied up before we left."

"Would it be alright if I sat in the sanctuary for awhile?"

"Certainly son. Will you make sure the door is locked on your way out?"

"Yes, I will, Pastor Ed. And thank you."

"Hank, it's good to see you. God be with you and Ben."

Hank walked into the colonial style sanctuary. He made his way halfway down the center aisle to the pew where he had spent so many Sunday mornings with his family. It was quiet, reverent, he closed his eyes unsure of what to pray or think.

Ben, where are you man? How did things come to this?

xxx

Hank's sleep was fitful. Ben had been worried the sheriff might think he murdered Susan and Tony, but just disappearing? It didn't seem right. It bothered him even more that Ben's car was in the driveway, the house

72

unlocked and his cell phone on the kitchen counter. More than anything, it bothered him that Ben's pack and rifle were missing.

His mind drifted to the last few weeks in the service.

Separating from the military during wartime was a strange mix of sweet and sour. Sweet because his active duty was done and he would not be returning to battle. Thank God for that! Sour because for better or worse he and Ben had developed a rhythm working together that would never be the same. Hank missed his friend every day.

In the morning, he made a call to John Cooper's office.

"John, this is Hank Murdoch."

"Hank, how are you? I heard you were coming in. Sorry it couldn't have been under better circumstances."

"Yeah, me too. Listen, John, do you mind if I come by to see you today?"

Cooper told Hank, barring any unforeseen circumstances, he would be back in the office in the afternoon.

At one-thirty, Hank pulled into the parking lot on Monroe Street, across from the Marion County Sheriff's Department, and walked through the glass panel double doors into the Sheriff's office.

The place looked like one might imagine a small county sheriff's office would be. There was an open space with a wooden counter centered half-way across the room. The walls were wood paneled half-way up with beige paint to the baffled drop-ceiling. There were several people sitting in wooden chairs along the walls of the waiting room. Behind a sliding glass window sat a secretary, talking on the phone.

"May I help you?" the woman asked, hanging up the

phone as she looked up.

"My name is Hank Murdoch. Sherriff Cooper is expecting me."

"Just a moment," she said picking up the phone.

"Sheriff Cooper? There is a Hank Murdoch here to see you."

She paused, listening, and then said with a smile as she pointed to the door, "I'll buzz you in, Mr. Murdoch."

As Hank stepped through the door, John Cooper came out of his office with a welcoming smile.

"Hank Murdoch!" he said, grabbing Hank's hand and pulling him in for a hug. "What a sight you are. You haven't changed one bit. Come on into the office."

Cooper's space, while smaller, had a similar look as the waiting room. Unlike the public area, it was filled with mementos. The large oak desk had two stacks of case files on one side and photos of his family on the other. Behind the desk on the wall Hank there was a framed picture of the Sheriff's friend and the Governor of West Virginia shaking hands. To his right a large window with venetian blinds halfway down, faced Monroe Street. A thin, closed file lay on the green ink blotter in the center of his desk. Hank could see that it said in block letters, MORRIS PARK MURDERS.

In front of the desk were two cushioned captain's chairs.

"Take a seat, Hank," said Cooper, sitting in one of the two. After talking a bit about their families, they spent a few minutes catching up on football memories.

"I'll never forget you taking out that blitzing linebacker from Elkins our senior year," Hank said, his mind playing back the action. "That guy had hurt more than one quarterback. That night, I thought he had me cold until he just disappeared from my field of vision!"

"Yeah," said John with a hearty chuckle. "I heard that asshole had been bragging he was gonna get you during the game."

"I heard it to," said Hank, chuckling right along with his old friend, "he had to sit out the next game because you practically broke his ribs!"

Hank saw John's gaze slip to the floor. They both sat silent for a few moments.

"Hank," said Cooper, his tone becoming more serious. "It's a damn shame about Susan Miller and Tony Cole. Over the years, we've had a murder or two, some suicides, and accidental deaths, but something like this? Here? This just doesn't happen."

"John," Hank said, his voice lowering. "I want to be honest with you. I came because Ben called me about the deaths."

"I wondered how you heard about it. I thought maybe your parents called you," Cooper said. Hank picked up an increased curiosity in the Sheriff's voice.

"You know Ben has disappeared. That's a problem." He continued, "He went to the morgue to make the positive ID, and nobody has seen him since. I stopped by his house yesterday to ask him a few questions. His car was in the driveway, but he didn't answer the door. I looked through the windows of the house and went over to the barn, but there was no sign of him."

The tone of his voice suggested he was frustrated.

"Obviously we just got started with the investigation, but everyone knows you and Ben trained as rangers and were a sniper team. If half of the stories you told me were true, you guys were killing machines."

Hank winced at John's out of context comments.

Very few would ever understand what it meant to hunt down and kill another human being. When his old friend said this, it sounded cold. It cut deep. He wished he had never said anything.

"Are you telling me, while it is early, Ben is your primary suspect," said Hank.

"At the moment, yeah," Cooper said, looking uncomfortable and gazing out the window. "Ben was my first thought and that of my team. Deputy Anderson brought the possibility up to me first thing at the crime scene."

The office got quiet again as the two men looked at each other. While it was not a surprise that Ben was considered a suspect, Hank realized Ben was John's only suspect.

Cooper, glanced up at his photo with the Governor and spoke first. "I'm don't want to jump to any conclusions, but at the moment, I have no alternative theories."

"John, you know Ben – we both know him. What would possibly be his motive?"

Cooper paused then looked straight at Hank, and said., "Okay, it's just conjecture, but everyone knows Ben and Susan had marital problems. You and I are both aware of their history even before they married. And Tony Cole was a snake in the grass."

He went on to tell Hank of the women in the community Cole had seduced. It was a long and unsavory list including coeds, female faculty and the University President's wife.

"And those are just the ones that are public knowledge and I know about. To be frank, I have no idea how Mary put up with him."

"Okay, John," Hank replied, wanting John to give

him more. "I get it. Tony chased any skirt that smiled at him. Why would Ben be the only person of interest? What about all the women he used? Their husbands? The College President?"

Hank watched his old friend sigh and run the fingers through his hair as if he were hoping a solution to the murder would suddenly appear, and all would be well.

Cooper continued, "It was no secret Tony and Susan flirted with each other over the years. God knows she seemed to be the only one he hadn't bedded. Finding them at night in a parked car at the reservoir did not look good."

"There could be a ton of reasons for them being there," Hank said. "And there could be other possibilities – a jealous husband, jilted lover. I mean the list could be pretty long."

"I agree, Hank, but it could also be that Ben was in an episode of PTSD and just lost it."

"Wait a minute, John," Hank said. "You know he underwent treatment. Dad counseled him and then referred him to the veteran's program in Morgantown. Do you know of any episodes he has had since he began treatment? By the way, how do you even know about this? I thought the records were sealed?"

"I began digging Friday and uncovered it this morning. I'm not saying anything here, I just need to take everything I can into consideration." John said.

Hank was irritated. "All I'm saying, John, is don't be jumping to conclusions." As soon as he said it he regretted the words.

"Don't tell me how to do my job, Hank. This is what I do for a living and I am pretty damn good at it. You might consider that the harder I push toward Ben, and if he is innocent, the quicker I'll find that out."

"You're right, John, I'm sorry I pushed so hard."

Changing the subject, he asked, "I know this isn't according to procedure, but are you able to share any of the evidence with me?"

Cooper seemed a little confused at the abrupt shift in conversation, but then said, "Share evidence? Well, this isn't evidence, but we've just started the murder book, mostly photos of the scene."

"Can I see them?" Hank pushed harder.

Hank saw Cooper's eyes go blank, like he was processing the questions and trying to decide how much to say. His eyes cleared, and he said, "Look Hank, I probably shouldn't have, but I shared some of the evidence with Ben before he disappeared. I feel like that might have been the reason he disappeared."

"I can't speak to that, but I'm not going anywhere." Hank said. "And I have a good investigation background. Maybe I can help.

He wasn't sure John was buying it, but then Cooper said, "The only pieces of hard evidence we have is a nine-millimeter shell casing and the slugs that hit Tony, which we recovered from the car. They were severely damaged from hitting the door. We reconstructed the trajectory in the shots that killed Susan, and found one slug in the ground about twenty feet from the passenger side of the car. It was in relatively good shape. We sent what we have to the FBI lab in Clarksburg for analysis. We couldn't find the other bullet. The casing the forensic team found the next morning was fourteen feet from the driver's side door. It went to the FBI too. Other than some footprints, there was nothing else."

Hank was curious. "Why do you think you only found one casing?"

"A couple of kids found the bodies. They said they were going to park at the pavilion for a *little private time*. We figure they scared off the killer before he could finish policing the brass."

"Were the footprints clean?" Hank asked, as his mind drifted into his years of tracking in the military.

"Hank, this is police business, you know –,"

"Listen, John," Hank interrupted, "You don't have to tell me anything more. You've already said quite a bit."

"Yeah, I know," he replied as Hank saw him glance at the file on his desk. "But since I've already started down the garden path, the boots were military treads, size eleven."

A chill ran up Hank's back. He knew Ben wore the same size.

Gathering himself, and hoping Cooper had not noticed anything, he said, "Any tire tracks other than Tony and Susan's cars?"

"Nothing – we found nothing else."

Hank left the Sheriff 's office and walked to a small coffee shop on Adam's Street. He needed to clear his mind. There was no way Ben could have, would have, killed Susan, but he knew a strong circumstantial case was being built.

Coffee in hand, he headed back to his car and sat for a few minutes. He decided if anyone could assess the murder scene, it would be him. Starting the car, he backed out of his space, pulled to the exit, turned right on Monroe Street, and headed for the Jefferson Street Bridge, across the river to Morris Park.

He could feel John Cooper watching him drive away.

CHAPTER 20

Fifteen minutes later, Hank pulled into the drive and up the hill into Morris Park. He followed the one-way road around the reservoir and when he arrived at the shelter, the crime scene tape had been removed. Apparently, the Marion County forensic team had completed their work. He didn't pull into the small parking lot but left his car on the other side of the road.

Something automatic took over. Years of tracking targets dictated that he work in a particular way. He knew scene investigation was a process involving all the senses.

He stood for a long time surveying the scene, observing carefully every square foot. There were the tire tracks of the two cars in the gravel parking area. One car had pulled in a little further than the other. The sets of tire tracks were five feet apart. Once the evidence had been gathered, the vehicles were removed, the crime-scene tape taken down and the area was cleared. By now there were footprints everywhere.

The area was surrounded on three sides by grass with woods all around the perimeter. The morning was warm and small beads of sweat began to form on his forehead. He undid a couple of buttons on his shirt and pulled it out of his trousers.

Staying outside the perimeter of the kill zone, Hank walked along the road above and below the entrance to the pavilion parking area.

An approaching car would have alerted Tony and Susan. The killer had to come on foot.

The shelter was the last one at the end of the one-way loop. Hank wondered whether the assailant might have walked up the hill from where the one-way loop began.

What would I have done?

He walked back down the hill to Pleasant Valley Road, crossed and stood in the parking lot of the Valley Lounge, thinking like a tracker.

The killing occurred at night. How could the guy know Tony and Susan would be there? How would he get to the park? How did he find them? If he drove, where would he hide the car?

Hank walked a little further along the road to a small foreign auto repair shop. It was just down the hill and past a slight bend. Looking back toward the park, he could not see the drive from the shop. He returned to the roadhouse parking lot. He walked up and down the outside edge of the gravel parking lot scanning it in sections. He stopped and stared at the driveway into the park on the other side.

He crossed the road to the entrance. He looked up and down the drive on the right side and then the asphalt road itself. He had just started scanning the the tree line to the left side of the road when he saw it. It looked as if someone had moved along the tree line. There were telltale signs of broken twigs and disturbed leaves. He tracked the trail staying on the drive, not wanting to disturb anything. Just before the small pavilion parking lot, it disappeared.

That's how the bastard got up the hill. Now I have to get behind the car.

He crouched and made his way past where the victims had been parked. Acting out the scene, he moved to a blind spot behind the car with Tony and Susan.

In his minds-eye, he drew a weapon, screwing a silencer onto its barrel. He crouched, as though he were the killer and quietly inched his way from behind the car to the driver's side window.

He raised himself, pointed a finger and said, "Pop, pop you're dead, Tony. Pop, pop, You're dead, Susan."

Three seconds max.

He stood still looking around.

What's next? Clean it up.

He scanned the ground in small concentric circles, moving further out two feet with each pass.

Four shots – one casing.

He mentally picked up three shells, then heard a car coming. Making a quick scan, he couldn't find the casing. Putting himself in the mind of the killer, he imagined the urgency.

Damn, where the hell is it. Where is it?

Concerned he might be seen, the shooter would not return to Pleasant Valley Road by way of the loop drive, he would go through the woods.

Hank walked around the parking lot, the pavilion and began to scan the tree line. At first, he didn't see anything, but then noticed a small, broken, low-hanging tree branch. From there he found a path of disturbed ground. It led down the hill through the woods. A little more than halfway, a larger area of the ground was disrupted.

He must have fallen.

It was then he saw something a few feet from the track. He stopped and looked. It was a small black plastic box not much bigger than a couple of Double A batteries side by side.

What the hell is that?

As he stared, he saw two concentric circles on one side of it. A flash of recognition. It was the size a small box with magnets.

It's a GPS tag! The killer tagged Tony's car!

Hank left the tracker where it lay. He knew once he called Cooper with what he had found, the Sheriff would send his team out again. He wanted to see whether they would find the unit and more importantly whether Cooper would tell him about it.

He didn't disturb the scene and continued to follow the trail down the hill. There was a ditch just past the tree line as he emerged to Pleasant Valley Road. It had a small amount of standing, muddy water. Crossing the road toward the Valley Lounge were two, pale light brown boot prints. He had missed them because he had walked in the other direction to the auto repair shop.

He crossed the road to the parking lot. It was empty, and the gravel looked undisturbed. Because of the murders, the owner closed the club through the weekend. The guy bitched about it, but did it anyway. As Hank got closer to the building, he noticed where a vehicle had pulled in on a dirt area on the side of the building. The tire tracks were crisp and deep, suggesting new tires. Cooper could check that out.

Is this where the shooter waited for his opportunity?

He pulled out his phone to call the Sheriff when an incoming text made it buzz in his hand. The ID read:

Unknown. His heart skipped a beat. On the screen, the words read: "Take the shot."

Ben was in contact.

CHAPTER 21

On the way back to town from Morris Park, Hank called Mary Cole.

He was hesitant. He had known Mary and dated her in high school. They also went out a time or two while he was on leave after his first tour in Afghanistan. He liked her, but circumstances in his life were too much for him to be seriously in pursuit. When he found out she married Tony Cole, he was disappointed he had missed the opportunity.

"Mary, this is Hank Murdoch. I called to say how sorry I am about Tony and Susan. I can't imagine how it must be losing your sister and husband like that. I just wanted you to know you were in my thoughts."

"Hank Murdoch?" She said. "What? Where are you calling from?"

"Here in Fairmont. I've been living in California for several years. I got a call from Ben three days ago, and I came right in."

"You're in Fairmont?" she said, sounding like she was still trying to get her mind around him calling her. "Oh, Hank, it's so good to hear your voice. I am still in shock. I don't understand any of this. Tony and Susan? None of it makes sense."

"I know this is a difficult time, but I wonder whether I might come over to see you."

"Uh. Of course. I would like that," Mary said, sounding as though she was getting her bearings. "Do you have a time in mind?"

Hank paused for a moment and said, "Change that. Why don't we have dinner this evening instead? We could go to Muriale's." He felt guilty at the pleasure the sound of her voice brought. "If we meet at five o'clock, it will be quieter, you know, before the dinner customers arrive."

"That sounds great. I'll see you there," Mary replied.

Hank headed home, took a shower and changed clothes. He was looking forward to seeing Mary. On his way to Muriale's, he felt a chill ripple through his body at the thought of seeing her again.

He pulled into the restaurant parking lot and waited. Punctual as usual, Mary arrived at five, parked her car, got out and walked toward the door of the restaurant.

Hank got out of his car.

"Mary, over here," he called as he jogged her way.

She was wearing a black collared, button-down shirt, blue jeans and a pair of sunglasses.

"Hank Murdoch," she exclaimed, taking off her sunglasses as she turned to look at him. "How great it is to see you!"

Walking across the parking lot, her auburn, shoulder length hair, flared then settled as she stopped in front of him. He hugged her, holding the embrace for a moment as he took in the sweetness of her freshly washed hair.

Stepping back, Mary said, "Oh, Hank, thank you for calling today. It was so good to hear your voice after all these years. Calming actually."

This was something Hank had never understood. His own life was drifting like a lifeboat fallen from a passing ship, and yet people in need were drawn to him. He didn't think he would ever get it.

As they walked into the restaurant, the smell of fresh bread, pizza, garlic and red sauce filled the air. Hank was taken back to the times he and Mary had come here. It felt good, and he was looking forward to the evening. The communication between them had always been relaxed. She was smart and he couldn't remember a time from junior high on, when he didn't feel an attraction. They had been an item for a couple of years. The sex was good, and they had a lot of fun. When their lives moved on they remained friends.

Because of the hour, they had their pick of the tables. Hank chose a two-top by the window overlooking the Tygart Valley River. The restaurant and the overhead music were quiet as they sat down.

The familiar and comforting ambiance of Muriale's turned on their hunger buds. The meal began with bruschetta and the locally famous cheese bread. Hank ordered his favorite – Tortellini, and Mary, spicy sausage rigatoni. He had a glass of Chianti Placido and she a California Cabernet. They both smiled when Hank reminded her of the times they had eaten Spaghetti here adding, "…because only good friends eat stringed pasta together in public."

"Tell me what you have been doing since the last time we saw each other," she said, sweeping back her hair.

Hank talked a little about the final years of his military experience. One of his challenges was no longer working with Ben. He told her that after trying a semester at Fairmont State, he found himself unsettled.

"I don't understand what it was like in the war,"

Mary said. "But I can appreciate it must have been a dramatic change to leave the service."

Returning to civilian life had not been as easy as he had thought. The short version, the only kind he told anybody, was that he attended junior college in San Diego. He then opened a small detective agency in Encinitas, California.

Always self-effacing, he continued that the agency had not grown much. He had a few cases from Fort Pendleton in Oceanside, but not enough to sustain him. To make ends meet, he ran an early morning 'ranger' boot camp exercise program. He said he was still sorting things out.

Hank gazed out the window, down the hill to the river, to a small fishing boat with a couple of youngsters casting their lines. She followed his eyes and absent-mindedly said, "Things were much simpler in those days, weren't they?"

He smiled and nodded, both lost in thoughts of another day and time.

Finishing the appetizers, and waiting for the entrée, Mary began to talk.

"It's really weird," she said. "Not only are Tony and Susan gone, but I found out that Tony's father Gus died of a heart attack the same night."

"Maybe it was the shock of hearing his son had been killed," Hank said.

"That's the thing. I heard they found him dead in his house when they went to tell him about the murders."

"That is really strange," Hank said getting a feeling that something wasn't right. "Did he have a bad heart?"

"I always thought he was a healthy man," she replied and looked out the window brushing her hair back. Then lowering her voice, she looked right at him.

"Hank, I couldn't say this to anyone else. My life with Tony was a living hell almost from the beginning. He was so charming, so kind, so gentle, but once we married it all changed. He became distant, preoccupied, and then rumors got back to me about the women."

Hank was surprised at her candor.

"Mary," he said, touching her hand. "You don't have to talk about this."

"No, Hank, I do, but if you are uncomfortable, we can change the subject."

"I am fine with it," he said, but felt like a voyeur peeking through a window into her personal life. "I just don't want you to feel you have to."

"I don't have to," she said. "I need to."

Mary went on to tell Hank how she found about the first woman. Tony came home late one night. He said he had been in Morgantown at his father's restaurant, but what she smelled on his clothes was not Italian red sauce, it was the musky, unmistakable odor of sex. She confronted him and he admitted he had been with an old girlfriend from high school. Tony promised it would never happen again. But it did happen again, and again, and again until he no longer tried to make excuses. In the beginning, the girls came from Morgantown, but then he began to chase married women and coeds in Fairmont. It became common knowledge and she was humiliated.

Hank felt the anger and frustration coming from her words. Her countenance had turned dark, her resentment coming from a deep and dark place. Rather than looking at him as she spoke, she stared out the window and then to the bar and back to the window.

"Why did you stay with him?" Hank asked,

genuinely curious.

"I don't really know," she said. "I guess I believed deep inside, I could reel Tony back in. Maybe it was stubborn Scottish pride from my mother."

In the beginning, she thought she could satisfy Tony's appetites, but in the end, they exceeded her ability to calm the beast. "As it turned out," Mary said, looking out the window again. "I overestimated my strength and underestimated Tony's."

Mary looked down at the table, pausing as though she weren't uncertain what to say. Listening to her, Hank felt himself being pulled into the darkness of her world.

She took a drink of wine, and lifted her head looking Hank directly in the eyes. "If you want to know the truth," she continued, the bitterness of bile in her voice. "I'm glad Tony is dead, and if he were having an affair with my sister Susan, they both can rot in hell."

CHAPTER 22

Mary's bitterness surprised Hank. When she finished, there was a silence lasting for some time. People often feel uncomfortable with sustained quietness, but Hank's military experience was all about patience and waiting. He said nothing, giving her space.

After her confession, the anger lifted, and Mary looked like a little girl that had lost her way. She took a deep breath as though she were trying to decide whether to say anymore. Hank waited. Mary gave him a weak smile and glimpsed out the window again. He watched her glance back at her food, pushing it around her plate as though she lost her appetite. She looked up, the Rigatoni barely touched.

"I had an affair, Hank."

"Mary, don't–"

"It was Clayton Anderson," she blurted out.

"John Cooper's deputy?" Hank exclaimed, trying to conceal his surprise

"Yes," she said.

He sat, stunned at this news.

"Several months ago," she related, "the house was broken into."

She explained that because she and Tony lived

outside of the city limits, it was the Sheriff's jurisdiction. The dispatcher sent Anderson to investigate. He was professional and checked everything before filing a report. He told her to call anytime she was concerned about security. After that, she saw him a couple of times in town.

One evening at the Middletown Mall, they bumped into one another. They talked for a while. Anderson said he knew about Tony's infidelities and told her he would never treat a woman that way.

"It was nice, you know?" She said, wistfully as she crossed her arms, leaning back against her chair. Running her fingers through her hair and sighing., "Nice to have a man make me feel appreciated."

Clayton and she met for coffee a time or two after that. One thing led to another, and they soon found themselves in a relationship.

"At first, I thought it was just a way for me to get back at Tony, but after a few weeks, I felt guilty, not because of Tony, but because it just wasn't right. We were hiding and meeting in secret. I couldn't take it." Hank saw her brown eyes darken. Looking away from him as she continued, "It was a hard break-up for Clayton. He felt protective of me, and hated Tony. He told me if Tony ever hurt me, he would kill him."

Hank didn't know what to think or say. He had called to console Mary. He liked her, and in all honesty, that was part of his motive for seeing her in person, but this was unexpected.

The rest of the evening was spent in awkward small talk. By the time Hank and Mary left Muriale's, it was nearly eight.

Hank walked her to her car, the humid river air cloaking everything with a fine mist.

"Hank, thank you for being with me tonight. I am sorry if this was too much for you, but just being able to talk freely has made me feel like a mountain was lifted off my shoulders. You are a good friend, and I am grateful you called today."

Maybe it was the alcohol, the confession or both, but Mary looked calm and relaxed. She reached out, stood on her toes and hugged him tightly, her arms around his neck and chest.

"I'm glad we were able to get together," he said, the evening's conversation and the woman in his arms weighing on his mind. He kissed her cheek and let her go.

"I know the coming days are going to be tough. If it's alright, I would like to keep in touch."

"I hope so," she said as she turned to get in her car.

As she drove off, Hank processed everything he heard over dinner. It was overwhelming and much more than he had anticipated. An evening meant for consolation and seeing an old friend, turned into a troubling confession.

Clayton Anderson had an affair with Mary Cole. He hated Tony Cole. He knew how to use weapons. Hank's mind was in overdrive.

Clayton had been a couple of years behind Hank in school, and he didn't know much about him. That was about to change.

CHAPTER 23

Hank pulled into the driveway at his parents' home and sat in the car. He reviewed what he knew about the killing from the Sheriff, his visit to Morris Park and dinner with Mary. His mind shifted into the hunt and track mode that had occupied so much of his military life.

"Hank?" Peter called out from the front porch. "Are you alright?"

His father's voice startled him. He responded, "I'm good, Dad. Just thinking."

"Your mother was a little worried that you were just sitting in the car," Peter said.

Hank got out and walked toward his father. "Dad, can I get on the computer in your office? There are a few things I would like to check out."

"Not a problem, son," Peter replied. "I'll give you the password."

Hank went inside and hugged his mother. After a few minutes chatting, he headed to his father's office where his dad had already turned on the computer and entered the security password. The code was written on a small piece of paper beside the keyboard.

Mary's revelations at dinner had come as a surprise.

He couldn't blame her for the feelings of humiliation, and could understand turning to another man. But he was blown away that it was the Deputy Sheriff Clayton Anderson.

Hank opened Google and typed *Clayton Anderson, Fairmont West Virginia.*

He didn't expect to find much about Anderson, but it was a place to start. Initially, his name appeared with a link to the Sheriff's office. There were some of the same pictures he had seen on the wall in the waiting area at Cooper's office. On the site was a short bio recounting the year he graduated from high school and a two-year vocational certificate in Criminal Justice.

Hank grunted when he saw the criminal justice thing. The course he had taken at the junior college in San Diego was probably similar, but for him, it was only a time filler. It appeared Anderson had gotten the associate's degree so that he could be in law enforcement.

It was the end of the bio that caught his attention. It indicated Clayton had been honorably discharged after five years in the military police. It seemed odd that Anderson would leave the army at five years. There must have been extenuating circumstances. Four and six-year enlistments were usual, but five? Hank made a note to follow-up. The rest of the bio was brief, ending with the comment he had been with the Sheriff's office since 2010.

Since Hank didn't know much about the military police or their training, he did a further search and discovered it consisted of training in Military Law, police tactics, battlefield forensics, communications and advanced map-reading skills. Maybe he should have known this after eight years in the military, but he and Ben were insulated by their work in the field. They never had occasion to interact with the MPs.

As he scrolled through the website pages, one thing caught his attention. The standard issue sidearm was a nine-millimeter Beretta.

CHAPTER 24

Hank took a small paper pad from the bookshelf by his father's desk and made notes of what he had learned. Despite the fact he did not believe Ben had done this, he tried to put himself in the Sheriff's mind. On the notepad, he wrote – *motive*, *means*, and *opportunity*.

Hank separated himself from his friendship with Ben as he began the process putting him at the top of the list.

Motive? Tony's conquests of women, single or married, were well known. Susan openly flirted with him. There had been trouble in Ben's relationship with Susan as long as they had been together. Their marriage had not changed that. She had been killed in Tony's car at night, parked at a pavilion at Morris Park. Tony's neck cut sent a signal that this was more than just a killing…PTSD triggered by jealousy?

Means? Ben no doubt had the skillset and tools to kill Tony and Susan. He was trained to kill efficiently. At the scene, a nine-millimeter shell casing was found, along with a size eleven boot print. Hank knew Ben had a nine-millimeter Beretta and the same size boot. The killing looked professional, from the standpoint of the closely grouped headshots. Hank and Ben had been trained to do these kinds of killings.

Opportunity? Jealousy is a slow burning candle. If Ben had been harboring this, he could easily have been keeping track of Susan's activities. It would have been easy for him to have checked with Janet Moore, or to have followed Susan that night. Killing Tony and Susan would have not have been difficult for someone like Ben and he could have returned home undetected before Cooper showed up at his door.

Even though Hank would never accept Ben as the killer, it would not have been difficult for Ben to track either Tony or Susan. His skills and patience would no doubt fit into the picture the Sheriff had begun to build.

Drawing a horizontal line below the notes he had made about Ben, Hank turned his attention to Clayton Anderson.

Motive? According to Mary, Clayton cared about her, maybe loved her, and had threatened to kill Tony if he harmed her.

Means? Clayton was a deputy with training that would allow him to track Tony and kill him, but how would Susan fit into this? Collateral damage? Maybe Clayton came upon them, saw the opportunity and took it, killing them.

Opportunity? If he had decided to kill Tony, he could easily keep tabs on him, follow and commit the murders.

As he sketched his thoughts, his mind returned to dinner with Mary. When she said she hated Tony, it came from some deep and shadowy place inside her. Maybe she conspired with Clayton, and the two of them planned the killing.

Hank drew another horizontal line and repeated the process with Mary as the potential suspect.

Motive? She hated Tony and could have killed him herself. Additionally, Clayton cared about her. She could easily have stoked the fires of his jealousy and encouraged him to murder for her. In spite of what she told him at dinner, maybe she actually wanted the deputy and eliminating Tony was the pathway.

Means? He wasn't sure about this yet, if she were to murder Tony and her sister by herself, she would need to have a weapon. Slashing Tony's throat? Possibly, but doubtful. If, on the other hand, she had pushed Clayton, it would not be a problem.

Opportunity? She could have followed Tony for some time. Seeing him with Susan, might have been just enough for her to go over the edge and kill them both.

The scenario regarding Mary didn't seem as plausible, but then *hell hath no fury as a woman scorned.*

An hour later, Hank felt like there wasn't much else he could do. He shut down the computer, said goodnight to his parents and headed for bed. Tomorrow would be another day.

Just as he closed the bedroom door behind him, his phone buzzed with an incoming text. He looked at the screen. It read – Latitude N 39.663515 and Longitude W -79.848045.

Ben had given Hank his location.

CHAPTER 25

Tuesday, June 17th

    Hank was up early in the morning. His parents were still sleeping when he made coffee, grabbed a cup and slipped out the front door. Notepad and the hot drink in hand, he walked along the short path to Ben's house and climbed the steps to the porch. He took a wooden chair facing the valley.

    The grayness of the emerging day gave everything a drab, two-dimensional look – the kind that causes the ground and trees to blend together with little or no distinction. He took a deep breath of the crisp morning air and wondered why he had ever left this place. The sweet scent of the pine and hardwood maple were energizing.

    As the rising sun behind him created an incremental carpet of light appearing across the Valley to the West, he cleared his mind and let the orchestra of waking woods and chirping birds pour in. Hank loved this time of day.

    Thirty minutes later, most of the valley was lush and green. Everything around Ben's house was now in sharp focus and full color. Hank had forgotten about the coffee and by the time he picked it up, it was cold, a fitting metaphor for the way he felt about this whole situation.

What the hell, Ben? Why go to ground? I thought we were going to work on this thing together.

After reviewing his notes from the night before he went down the steps and headed to the barn. Since Saturday, when he and his father were here, he knew he needed to come back alone. Inside the building, he walked over to the ladder and climbed to the loft. He went directly to the cabinet, turned the combination dial and opened the doors.

Taking a quick inventory, he noted everything Ben needed for survival was gone from the cabinet – weapons, MREs, Bivy tent and other survival gear. He checked the coordinates Ben had sent the night before. It was in a small neighborhood near Cheat Lake. Hank knew Ben would not be camped there, but was probably somewhere in the state forest. He would wait for more.

Closing the doors, Hank climbed down the ladder and out of the barn. Nobody knew he and Ben had gathered and stored the paramilitary equipment, and if he could help it, nobody would.

"What's going on, son?" came his father's voice. He was standing beside the steps of Ben's porch as Hank came out of the barn. Hank had been in deep thought and was startled by the sound of his Peter's voice.

"Morning, Dad," Hank replied as he walked toward him. "I woke up early and thought I would come over here and sit on the porch to clear my head. All of this has been overwhelming."

"When I got up, I smelled the coffee, but you were nowhere to be found. I thought you might be over here," Peter said.

Hank smiled and hugged his father. This was another thing he had missed. While he might not have measured up to Peter's expectations for his life, the love of the Murdoch family was strong and deep.

"Let's head back to the house and grab some breakfast. Mags is up and itching to make you some buckwheat pancakes."

"Great idea," Hank replied, as memories of the taste and smell of his mother's morning offering filled his mind. He grabbed his empty cup and notepad from the porch and headed home with his father.

CHAPTER 26

After breakfast and a quick shower, Hank called John Cooper. He knew John would be guarded, but hoped he could trade a little information with him.

"John Cooper," came the familiar voice.

"John, Hank here. Do you have a little time today? There are a couple of things I would like to show you."

"Hank, yeah, my morning is actually pretty free. What do you have in mind?"

Hank felt the caution in his friend's voice. He sensed he would need to be careful when playing this out, giving John a little bit and seeing how things unfolded. He wanted to bring Clayton Anderson into the equation but knew it would have to be done delicately.

"I went up to Morris Park yesterday. I wanted to get a feel for the scene. I was going to just look around, but the police tape had been taken down, so I poked around the whole site. I noticed a few things that might be of interest to you."

Hank was careful not to give the impression he was interfering with Cooper's investigation. He absolutely did not want him to think he was trying to deflect attention away from the focus on Ben – yet. What he wanted was to expand John's peripheral vision on the case.

"We've already given the area a pretty thorough going over Hank," John said, sounding confident.

"I was pretty sure you had, but wondered if your guys had noticed anything interesting along the tree line at the edge of the open area, away from the pavilion?" Hank asked, trying to sound casual.

"Hang on a minute," John said, his voice a little patronizing.

The phone got silent for a few moments. Hank waited, as John checked with his team. When he came back on the phone, he sounded irritated.

"I can head up there now and meet you. Will that work?" Cooper asked, emphasizing the question, as though it were a pain for him to do this. Hank knew by Cooper's tone of voice that his people had not expanded their search beyond the perimeter of the parking lot and pavilion.

"I just finished breakfast with Mom and Dad. I can be at the park in a half hour. I'll see you there."

Thirty minutes later, when Hank arrived, he saw the Marion County Sheriff's Chevy SUV sitting in the gravel parking area. Cooper was walking along the tree line as if he were trying to see could find anything. While he was a good sheriff, he was not a tracker and did not know what to look for.

Hank parked and made his way over to his friend.

"Hank, I don't see shit over here. I've walked this area three times, and it looks to me like a normal group of trees."

Hank didn't want to belittle John. "Yeah, I didn't see anything either on the first pass, but then I noticed this broken branch over here," pointing to a spot a few feet from where there were standing.

He took Cooper to the place where the killer had entered the woods. Once he showed him the spot, the sheriff saw it right away.

"Follow me," he said entering the brush. "Careful coming in here but see where the ground has been disturbed."

"Damn!" exclaimed John. "You must have done a lot of this when you were in the military. I never would have seen this if you hadn't pointed it out."

They headed down the hill through the woods, coming out on Pleasant Valley Road a little north of the entrance to the park. They jumped the narrow water drenched ditch and stepped to the side of the road.

"Look at this, John," Hank said, pointing to the dried muddy footprints on the pavement pointing toward the Lounge.

The Sheriff let go a long, "Sheiiit!" and pulled his phone from his pocket.

"Clayton," he said, as someone on the other end answered. "I need you to get your forensic team back out to Morris Park ASAP. We missed some things. I'll show you the area where you need to look. Any word from the FBI lab on the slug or shell casing?"

Clayton apparently indicated there was nothing yet. "See if you can push them to fast track it," the Sheriff said.

Hank saw the frustration on John's face. He knew he would need to lead, not push him.

Cooper hadn't said anything about Hank to his deputy and that suited him just fine. After the Sheriff hung up, Hank wanted to be assured he would be kept out of any discussions regarding his involvement.

"I would prefer you kept me out of this. The last

thing you need is for your people to think I am getting into your business. Cops never like that."

John blew out a breath. "You're right," he said. "If we weren't good friends and you hadn't had the military background, I wouldn't have met you here. I respect you, Hank, but let's be careful with this."

Hank saw his friend pause, glance up the hill and then focus on him. "Look, I know you and Ben were real close. I don't know how you couldn't be after all that time together. Hell, we were all friends so I'm telling you I don't like how this is shaping up. Ben is beginning to look better and better for this. I wanted to say it out loud so we understand ourselves."

"I get it, John," Hank said in a serious tone, "But you know I don't believe Ben killed them, and I'm going to look and listen to see if there is an alternative possibility."

"I know that, Hank," his friend said. "If you find anything at all that will help us, I am open to it. As long as you come to me with anything you find, I'm good."

"You've got it, man," Hank replied, looking John in the eyes. "Anything I find is yours and yours alone."

That was just what Hank hoped for. Now that John's team was coming back on the scene, he was confident they would do a more thorough search of the entire area. He was also sure they would find the GPS tracker unit. If Cooper shared that piece of evidence with him, he would know the Sheriff was holding nothing back.

Hank then took Cooper across the road to the Valley Lounge parking lot and showed him the tire tracks where a car had recently parked.

"I think this is where the killer waited and watched until he was sure Tony and Susan were in the park,"

Hank said.

"Maybe so," Cooper said. "The team will take a closer look."

Hank sensed there wouldn't be any resistance from John. He now felt he had the trust he needed to approach the Sheriff with an alternate theory of who might have done this. Clayton Anderson and Mary Cole were climbing to the top of his list.

The men walked back up the hill on the road so they wouldn't disturb the woods any more than they had. Cooper said he was going to wait for his forensic team to come. They headed to Hank's car and shook hands. Hank was getting in when Cooper said, "You know what is strange? I got a call from Sheriff Trach in Morgantown Friday afternoon. Deputy Anderson called him to notify Cole's father. He sent one of his men to the house. The door was unlocked, the television on and Mr. Cole dead in his easy chair."

CHAPTER 27

By the time Hank left Cooper at the park it was 10 o'clock in the morning. He was just heading back into town when his phone buzzed again with a text message: *Today – Noon!* Ben had sent him all he needed.

Instead of taking the Fairmont Connector back to town, he turned toward Interstate 79. He could be at the Cheat Lake coordinates in 30 minutes.

On the drive north, his mind was moving so quickly thoughts were coming in paragraphs emerging in his consciousness like jumping fish chasing insects on a summer's pond.

Ben was not a murderer. He didn't care what Cooper thought. He knew his friend better than anyone. Crisis management? They practiced it every day in the war. It was always a matter of life and death during their tours. Killing Susan and Tony Cole in a wildfire of jealousy was not his friend and partner. As much as he loved that woman, Ben would have walked away before killing her.

Then there was Mary Cole. Two things emerged from dinner the night before. While Hank cared about Mary, he could imagine a scenario where she had used Anderson to kill Tony. In this situation, when the opportunity presented itself, Susan would have been collateral damage.

What about the affair Tony had with Sally Jenkins, the College President's wife? Would he have had the resources to murder Tony for ruining his marriage, and publically humiliating him?

Passing Morgantown on his way north, something in his subconscious tugged at him. He couldn't quite find it, but it was something Cooper had said. He tried a couple of times to get to it, but let it go. His thoughts focused on the excitement of seeing Ben.

Two miles south of Cheat Lake his phone rang.

"Hank, here," he said.

"How far out are you?" It was Ben.

"Jesus, Ben," Hank exclaimed, his heart starting to pound.

"We'll talk later. How far are you out?"

"A couple of clicks from the coordinates."

"Good," Ben said. "I'm not there. Take exit 15 to County Road 73 to the Cooper's Rock Park entrance. Head up the drive 200 meters and park in the pullout. I'll meet you there."

The phone went dead.

Three minutes later, Hank left the Interstate and turned on the State road toward the park. Following Ben's instructions, he parked his car, got out and waited.

"Hey, brother," came the sound of the voice as much a part of him as his own.

Hank turned to see his friend emerge from the trees in camouflage dress. They embraced, and stepped apart.

"Damn, man," Hank said, full of emotion, "It is great to see you."

Ben put his finger to his lips and looked around. "Follow me." Leading him through the woods to a small clearing, he stopped to face his friend.

Before Ben could say anything, Hank said, "Man, what the hell made you take off? How did you get here? Where are you camping out?"

"Slow down, man," Ben replied. "One step at a time."

Ben relayed what happened Friday morning after he called Hank. "The more I thought about it, I realized it would not be a difficult leap that I killed them. I mean, look at the facts. Susan always flirted with Tony. The guy slept with every woman he could, and the two of them were at Morris Park, at night, alone in Tony's car," Ben said. "I mean, if you didn't know me, what would you think?"

"There is not a doubt the killings were professional. You and I did a lot of this sort of thing. It wouldn't take a genius to think I had murdered them out of jealousy."

Hank listened as Ben re-counted his decision to find the killer, and his fear that if he got picked up, the trail would go cold and there would be no way to prove his innocence.

"Yeah, you can imagine my surprise when I got home Saturday afternoon and you were gone. It was pretty damn strange. Your car was in the driveway, house open and cell phone on the kitchen counter. It was like you evaporated."

When Ben told him how he made the decision to disappear, his preparations and the way he got out of Fairmont, Hank was impressed. Hank was even more impressed Ben had contacted Dequan, an African American man in one of the more dangerous towns in Northern West Virginia.

CHAPTER 28

Ben and Hank sat on the ground with their backs against two maple trees a few feet apart. This was their custom when tracking. It was a habit allowing them to watch each other's back.

"Dequan Terry?" Hank said, chuckling. "The guy you played summer league ball with in high school? Christ, Ben, nobody would ever make that connection. And Osage? A white boy getting help in that town? That was brilliant."

The moment of humor was quickly replaced by a sense of urgency. They knew they were going to have to work swiftly, and Hank would need to provide the Sheriff with an alternative scenario.

"Let me catch you up on what I know," Hank said.

He told Ben about the meeting at Cooper's and the subsequent trip to the crime scene at Morris Park. "John's forensic team is not incompetent, just not experienced in this sort of thing. They never thought to expand the crime scene to the edge of the pavilion park, and tracking is not what they are trained to do. I think Cooper was embarrassed they missed the killer's egress trail."

Hank was sure he understood how the killer tracked

Tony, but didn't know for how long. "I saw a GPS lying in the woods heading down the hill. I didn't touch it. I left it for Cooper's team to find."

He continued. "I think the guy followed Tony to Morris Park last Thursday night. When Tony drove into the park the killer parked beside the Valley Lounge and waited, thinking he would maybe get him somewhere on his way home. When Susan turned in, he didn't think anything about it until she did not come out. I'm pretty sure the guy got out, walked up the entrance drive on foot, found them in Tony's car and shot them."

It was quiet in the clearing, the small open area in the forest like a cathedral at a time of prayer. Except for the two men talking, it was silent and still.

"I'm pretty sure Tony was the target and Susan happened to be in the wrong place at the wrong time," Hank concluded.

"Who the hell would have done this," Ben said, staring off into the woods.

"That's the question, isn't it? One thing we know for sure, it wasn't you."

Hank then told him about his dinner with Mary Cole. "She was demeaned by Tony over and over. She admitted she hated him. I totally get that. Then she told me she had an affair with Clayton Anderson, one of the Sheriff Deputies. Do you remember that guy from high school?"

"Yeah, I've seen him around," Ben replied. "So, what?"

"The 'so what,' is that when she broke it off, he told her if Tony did anything to hurt her, he would kill him."

A small breeze moved through the trees at the edge of the clearing, causing the men to look around to make sure they still were alone.

When Hank glanced back at Ben, he saw a shift in his friend's expression. His blue eyes were blank, like he was gazing into the universe. His face was expressionless. It was a look he recognized. When he and Ben had begun to close in on a target, there was a focus that shut everything else out, like the athlete who no longer hears the cheering crowd. He also felt himself shift into another gear.

He re-counted his background check on Anderson.

"Turns out he was an MP for five years, honorably discharged early. I don't know why yet. I did some searching on MP training. They get time in standard and electronic tracking and are issued nine-millimeter Beretta pistols. Cooper told me a nine-millimeter did the killing."

"So, do you make Anderson for the murder?" Ben asked.

"I'm not sure yet," replied Hank. "But he sure looks better for it than you."

Hank reviewed possibilities of motive, opportunity and means for the Deputy and Mary Cole. He also suggested the possibility that Mary hired someone else. Finally, he talked about the College President who had been cuckolded, by Tony.

"I wouldn't consider the college guy very seriously," Ben said after he heard Hank's thoughts. Hank agreed but wanted to explore every possibility he could.

Both understood Hank was going to be the guy out front. As Hank got ready to leave, Ben said, "I'm not telling you where I'm camped. It's better that you can honestly say you don't know."

"I get it," Hank replied with a nod and knowing look.

Ben reached into his pocket and pulled out one of

the disposable phones he had taken with him. He gave Hank the number of the phone he was carrying and said, "This will keep our communication off the grid."

As Hank turned to leave, he said, "You know what's strange? Cooper told me that Tony's father died of a heart attack the same night of the killings. I think that's a weird coincidence."

They looked at each other – neither one of them believed in coincidence.

CHAPTER 29

It was still early in the afternoon, so on his way back to Fairmont, Hank stopped for lunch at the China City Restaurant in Morgantown. He picked up some fresh food from the buffet and headed for a table.

The death of Tony's father bothered him. He opened his phone and Googled funeral homes in Morgantown. There were four. The first two did not a have Gus Cole, but on the third call, he got lucky.

"Hastings Funeral home" answered a man with a sensitive-sounding voice. "How may we help you?"

Hank said he was a friend of Gus Cole and wondered when the memorial service would be held.

"Yes, Mr. Cole is with us. The formal viewing begins this evening at seven o 'clock. The main service will be the day after tomorrow at nine o'clock in the morning at St. Mary's Church. The family wanted it this way to allow people to come in from out of town."

"Thank you," Hank said, "I wonder whether I might stop by this afternoon to pay my respects."

"Of course," the man replied.

When Hank arrived, the somber looking gentleman at the door of Hastings directed him to the room where he would find Gus. There were flowers, an open casket and a few staff. He paid respects to the man in the coffin and noted a vaguely familiar face. The woman was tall, with gray hair and looked to be in her late sixties. She wore black trousers with matching jacket over a white open collared blouse. One of the funeral home employees was chatting with her.

Hank waited until she was free then walked up to her.

He said, with genuine empathy, "Mrs. Cole, I'm Hank Murdoch from Fairmont. I am sorry about the death of your husband and son. This must be unbearable for you."

She looked up and looked at him. ""Hank Murdoch," she said as a smiled crossed her face. I'm not Marilyn Cole. I'm Ann Stout, her sister. If I recall correctly, you and I met at Tony and Mary's wedding several years ago. It was during the rehearsal dinner at the Red Cellar."

"Of course," said Hank, a little embarrassed. He returned the smile as the memory flickered in his mind.

Glancing at the casket and back to Hank, she said, "This is a terrible series of events. Marilyn died last year, and with the murder of Tony there wasn't anyone to manage arrangements for Gus. I came down from Waynesburg to make sure everything would be taken care of."

The color of the walls was subdued, with lighting turned down enough to soften the edges of everything in the room. The acoustic tiled ceiling and carpeted floor absorbed the sounds of workers doing last minute preparations. The flowers around the casket filled the air with a sweetness that contradicted the purpose for which rooms like this were used. Hank had never liked these places.

After chatting for a few moments, he said, "Mrs. Stout, would you be willing to have coffee with me before the formal view begins this evening?"

"I'm not sure I understand," she said pushing her hair behind her right ear, a look of mild confusion on her face.

"I am a close friend of Ben Miller," he said. "He is a suspect in the killing of Tony and Susan." Hank looked to see Ann's reaction. She didn't show any change in expression, so he continued. "He and I served together in Iraq and Afghanistan for several years. I just do not believe he killed Tony or Susan."

"I still don't understand," she repeated, a small furrow showing on her brow.

"I think it's strange that Tony and his father both died last Thursday evening. I don't have anything clear in my mind, but was hoping maybe we could talk a little."

The woman hesitated as if she were considering the final funeral details she needed to coordinate.

"All right, Hank," she said, her face relaxing. "I don't know what I can offer. I need to finish the arrangements here, but I can be free in a half hour. How about meeting at the Boreman Bistro? It's two blocks from here on High Street."

"Thanks, Ms. Stout," he replied, feeling genuinely grateful.

"Please call me Ann."

"See you soon, Ann."

Hank wondered what he might learn from this woman. It might not be much, but he knew from experience, the best intel often came from the most unexpected places.

CHAPTER 30

When Ann Stout arrived, Hank was already seated at a small table.

"Ann, over here." Hank stood and waved his hand.

When she got to the table, he pulled back the chair for her. She smiled, "The reports that chivalry is dead, are apparently premature." They chuckled as she sat down.

After getting her a tall latte, he repeated condolences for the death of her sister the previous year, and for the task of managing the arrangements for Gus. They chatted briefly about each other's lives, before Hank said, "I was told Mr. Cole died of a heart attack. Apparently, Sheriff Trach found him at home, when he went to tell him about Tony's murder."

With a curious look on her face, Ann said, "It is odd. Gus was as healthy as a horse. I could imagine him dying from an accident, even murdered by one of his ex-employees," she said with a smile. "But a heart attack? I would not have guessed that."

"Can you tell me a little about him?"

Ann sipped her latte, took a breath and began. "When Gus inherited the restaurants from his father Bill, he grew them considerably. He also created the most successful catering business in the city. He eventually got a contract with the university, beating out three or four national companies. He was a tough businessman, and knew every part of his work. He was fair, but if you crossed him, you were done. He didn't believe in second chances. He was a demanding man. After Tony was born, Gus got more and more absorbed in work. Marilyn and he were partners in the business. She got an accounting degree at the university and kept Gus's books until two years before she died. The last couple of years, the cancer took its toll and she didn't have the energy anymore. "

"I'm sorry for asking this," Hank interrupted, "but was he abusive to her?"

"Oh, no," she said. "Just harsh. Marilyn and I used to tease that it must have been his Sicilian blood. He loved that woman and never raised a hand to her. "

"I thought Tony had Italian heritage, but I didn't know he was Sicilian," said Hank.

"Gus's father came to America when he was a young boy," Ann said, her eyes unfocused as though she were turning mental tumblers to open a lockbox of memories. "Funny thing about Gus's father, Bill. My sister, Marilynn, said he never talked about his background and would get angry if he were pressed about it. In the last few years of his life though he got Alzheimer's and Marilyn used to help out with day to day care when she could. As the disease progressed he became fearful, very upset and frequently ranted about a Mafia killing and having to disappear from Philadelphia. 'They're gonna find me, torture me and kill all of us – the whole family!'" Marilyn told me he sometimes yelled, eyes wild with fear and he would start talking Italian! Italian of all things."

A little smile turned the corners of her mouth. "Bill had no discernible accent, so Marilyn said they were all surprised when he spoke it. Sometimes he would accuse his wife, Sandy, of seeing other men and hiding his money. It was a difficult time for the family."

"Their family doctor told her this was common in older people and prescribed medicines that calmed him down. This was before we knew about Alzheimer's. As we looked back, Marilyn and I were pretty sure that's what he had. He died a miserable death, and in the end, didn't know anything or anybody."

Ann shifted in her seat, sipping a little more of her latte and taking a moment as if she were recalling the difficulties her sister and Gus encountered in caring for the elder Cole.

They talked for a little while longer about the arrangements for Gus. Both Tony and Gus would be cremated. Mary Cole had told Ann she would bring Tony's ashes to be buried with his father.

Hank thanked her for being so generous with her time, and asked if he could be of any help.

"No," she said. "Thank you, Hank. I didn't realize I needed to talk about this to someone. It was helpful for me, too."

As she got up from the table, she continued, "I really hope it wasn't Ben who killed Tony. I can't imagine how or why he could kill his own wife and brother-in-law."

With that she was out the door.

CHAPTER 31

Hank sat at the table for the next thirty minutes lost in thought. He still struggled with the idea that the murder and death of Tony and Gus on the same night was just a fluke. He picked up his phone and punched in a number. He got John Cooper's voicemail.

"John, Hank here. I'm in Morgantown. After you mentioned that Tony's father died the same night as Tony, I started thinking. Is it possible to find out if Gus Cole had an autopsy, and whether you could get a look at the report? I'll tell you more later."

Hank disconnected, got up and headed to his car. Once inside, he called Ben.

"Yeah," a quiet and nondescript, cautious sounding voice answered.

"Ben, it's me. I've had an interesting afternoon. I grabbed lunch in Morgantown and got to thinking more about Tony and his father both dying last Thursday. I decided to dig around a little."

He let Ben know that it had been easy to find the funeral home where Gus Cole's body was. He then told about him about his conversation with Ann Stout and her surprise that Gus's death had been ruled a heart attack.

"What I found most interesting was when she talked about Gus's father, Bill. Gus inherited the business when the old man began to falter. In the end, the old man became demented and frequently ranted about a murder in Philadelphia in the old days. He seemed frightened, that someone was looking for him and would kill him."

"What's the point?" Ben asked.

"What if Gus didn't die of natural causes? What if he was murdered too, and the scene of the crime made to look like a heart attack?" Hank continued.

"You're saying there might have been a triple killing last Thursday night?" Ben said.

"I don't know, I'm saying it's a possibility."

Hank ran down his list of suspects again with Ben.

"You're thinking it's possible the killing was unrelated to anyone you've already considered?" Ben said in a voice that let Hank know he was engaged and processing.

"Yeah, it is conceivable. From the people on the list, I like Clayton Anderson by himself, possibly colluding with Mary Cole, but we need more information," Hank said. "I called Cooper to see whether he could find out if there had been an autopsy on Gus Cole. His death is still an open question. Cooper didn't answer, so I left him a voice mail."

They spent a few minutes of small talk, before hanging up. Hank had almost forgotten how good it was to hear Ben's voice, even more so to be engaged in a hunt again.

As he pulled on to Interstate 79, his personal cellphone rang. He looked at the screen. It was Cooper.

He punched the talk button. "John, thanks for calling back."

"I got your message you were in Morgantown and wondered about Tony's father. An autopsy? I don't get it."

Hank began, "When you told me Tony and Gus died the same night, you said it was a weird coincidence. A voice inside my head sounded an alarm. That voice kept me alive chasing targets in the war. When I hear it, I listen. So, I decided to do a little checking."

He told John about finding the funeral home where Gus had been taken, meeting Ann Stout, and their conversation about Gus and his father, Bill Cole.

"I don't have a clear picture in my mind, but I am curious to see whether there might be any reason to suspect foul play." He hesitated, because the next thing he was about to say, would open a door of suspicion that would not easily be closed.

"You told me this morning that if I had any thoughts about who might have killed Tony and Susan, we should talk," he said. "Well, I do and I want to talk to you."

"Go ahead, I'm listening," the Sheriff replied.

"No, John, I want to talk to you in person. Do you think we can meet for coffee or dinner?"

It was Cooper's turn to pause. Hank felt if this door were opened, he and John would be all in.

"Okay, Hank," John said. "You know my dad's place, on the river in Colfax? Meet me there at seven this evening. We can talk and it will be private."

"Thanks, John. See you then."

This was Hank's one shot to bring John on board. He made the decision and was going to take it.

CHAPTER 32

Ann Stout walked back to the funeral home and spent the evening greeting people at the viewing for Gus. She stood by the casket, and shaking hands with the visitors after they had a few moments viewing the body. She graciously accepted condolences and thanked them for coming. With her sister, Marilyn, gone and Tony recently murdered, Ann was the only family member there to receive Gus's personal and business friends. They were one and the same. Gus never had time to cultivate personal relationships outside of work.

Like Hank, Ann never liked these places. The stands of fresh flowers, each with their own scents, created a sweetening sick atmosphere in the room. The low ceiling, subdued lighting and soft piped in organ music made everything feel closed in. Small groups of people chatted quietly around the edges of the room. Nobody sat in the five rows of folding chairs that had been provided.

She had been greeting visitors for some time, when she saw Mary Cole walk through the door. She was surprised. Ann and Mary did not know each other well, but had managed to spend time together at family events. Ann knew that Gus disapproved of his son's marriage to her. It wasn't anything personal, but he wanted Tony to marry a Roman Catholic girl from Morgantown, not some small-town Protestant. He knew of Tony's wandering eye and thought he could keep closer tabs on him if he lived in town and attended the same parish.

"Mary, I didn't expect to see you here this evening," Ann said. Realizing she sounded abrupt, she gently smiled. "Not that I gave it much thought. I know you're so busy with Tony's death. It didn't occur to me you might show up. Thank you so much for coming."

Ann stepped forward and reached out to Mary. The two women hugged. "I am so sorry about Tony," Ann said. Mary looked at the floor and took a deep breath and sighed.

"I thought I would come out of respect for Gus," she said, glancing around the room. Mary looked drawn and tired. She did not look like she was dressed for a funeral visitation. She wore blue jeans, a white shirt with sleeves just below the elbow and a light multicolored sleeveless vest. Her auburn hair was pulled back into a ponytail, held in place by a rubber band.

"Actually that's not true," Mary continued, looking a little nervous, like she just realized where she was. "I have been sitting around doing nothing since the shooting. I needed to get out of the house. I got in the car, started driving and found myself here. Tony will be released by the Medical Examiner tomorrow, and I'll be doing the same thing for him that you are doing for Gus. There was no way I could handle both funerals. I really appreciate your doing this, Ann."

They made small talk for a few minutes. Ann was surprised how comfortable she felt with Mary, though her conversation with Hank was still on her mind.

"Mary," she said, glancing around the mostly empty room. "Did Tony ever talk about his grandfather Bill

Cole?"

"I'm not sure what you mean," Mary replied.

"Let's sit down for a few minutes. I've been standing for over an hour. My feet could use a rest," Ann said as she made her way to a chair on the end of the first row.

The women sat beside each other looking at the casket for a few moments.

Turning to Mary, Ann took her hand and began, "This is a really tough time for us, especially for you. I asked about Gus's father because Hank Murdoch came by here this afternoon. We chatted for a few minutes and then met for coffee. We talked about a number of things, but he was particularly interested in Gus's death. That led to a conversation about Bill Cole, Gus's father. It brought up a lot of memories for me."

At the sound of Hank's name, Ann noticed Mary stiffen. "We talked about my sister Marilyn, Gus's wife, and their relationship in the family business." Ann continued. "That's when we got into talking about Bill and the last years of his life. I found myself repeating some of the stories Marilyn told me Bill talked about before he died."

"Yes," Mary said. "When Tony and I were dating, he bragged about his grandfather. He liked to say, even though his name was Cole, he came from Sicilian heritage. He said, his grandfather was a tough guy and had come from out east somewhere."

Ann said. "I heard similar things from Marilyn too. As the Alzheimer's was taking Bill's life, he told stories about being a criminal when he was young and a gang killing. To be honest, we didn't put much stock in them."

"I probably can't add much," Mary said. "Tony

made a lot of things up to impress people – women mostly. He mentioned his grandad had been in the Mafia once. I chalked it up to big talk. Tony did a lot of that. He would say whatever he thought would get him what he wanted. When I asked him how he knew that, he fumbled around with some nonsense answer about it being a family secret."

"I'm not sure about *a family secret*," Ann said. "None of us had an inkling that any of it was true."

The women chatted a little longer before Mary said, "I should be heading home. I've been so keyed up. Just talking to you has helped me relax a little. I didn't realize how exhausted I am."

"I'll be done here in another hour or so. If you need anything, please call," Ann said as they stood and hugged. She watched the young woman leave the room, hoping Mary would have enough energy for the drive home.

xxx

Mary was tired, but not too tired to drive. The conversation with Ann created some anxiety and with that, a burst of energy. As she pulled out of the parking lot of the funeral home, She reached for her phone in her purse and speed-dialed a number she had not deleted nor used for several months.

"Hello," came the familiar voice.

"Clayton, we need to talk."

CHAPTER 33

After the viewing was over, Ann decided to go back to Waynesburg. It wasn't that far, and while she had booked a room at the Hotel Morgan she wanted to sleep in her own bed. Tomorrow would be a busy and emotionally draining day.

Her mind was active on the drive. She opened the windows to breathe in the mountain air. There were things she had not told Hank that afternoon, and even though Mary didn't add much, talking to her about Tony and his grandfather, caused one of Marilyn's stories to bubble to the surface of her mind.

xxx

In the last years of Bill Cole's life, it wasn't just a few rantings in Italian or outbursts of fear that someone would kill him and the family. Bill told stories – lots of stories. He said his name wasn't Bill Cole, but Biaggio Calegaro from Philadelphia. He talked about being an immigrant from the old country, how he had killed a mob boss and how he got to West Virginia. They sounded like adventures from gangland novels or movies like the Godfather or Capone. The reason they appeared fantastic is that they were so opposite of the Bill Cole everyone, including his family, knew.

During those times his wife, Sandy, listened and held his hand. "It's alright darlin'. You're safe. We're safe." In time, he was placed in a home where Sandy visited him almost every day watching the man she loved drift into darkness and incoherence. During that time, Marilyn helped Sandy with Bill. She spent several hours on weekends with her father-in-law to give Sandy time and space for herself.

Marilyn didn't know whether these accounts were accurate, or just the imaginations of an old man with dementia. True or not, over time, she pieced together an account that was fascinating. She shared everything she heard with her sister Ann.

This was occupying Ann's mind on the drive home.

CHAPTER 34

After listening to so many descriptions of her father-in-law's so-called early life, Marilyn told Ann what she thought. "This is the best I can tell after hearing all of this," she began.

According to Bill, his family had come from Palermo, Sicily and arrived in New York in 1910 when he was two. He was named Biaggio after his father Joseph's brother. His parents had planned a large family in their adopted country but his birth had been difficult and his mother Alessa was unable to have any more children. Like a lot of immigrants, his father, a stone mason, couldn't find work in the City, so he moved his young family to a tenement house in Philadelphia. There he took a job as a laborer.

In the beginning, Biaggio enjoyed school and was a good student but had a temper. In the eighth grade, he was expelled for fighting and never returned. By his mid-teens, he was in a street gang involved in petty theft. At twenty-one, he joined the Lanzetta family, a small piece of the city's Mafioso.

Marilyn Cole had done some research and discovered there was such a mob family in Philadelphia around the time of Bill's stories. The Italians who came to this country found a lot of discrimination, and formed close-knit neighborhood families. Many of the men who came to America had Mafia connections from the old country.

xxx

In Philadelphia, the Mafia grew under the leadership of Salvatore Sabella, a street thug who pulled together a fledgling group of young Italian immigrants. Jobs were scarce, so recruiting these men for an organization was not a problem. He held power until 1927 when John "Big Nose" Avena, a Sicilian, took over the organization.

In 1932, hoping to take over the Philadelphia organization, Leo Lanzetta made a move and sent some of his boys to murder Avena. The killers were Harry Riccobene, Alonzo Casella and twenty-four-year-old Biaggio Calegaro.

Several efforts to kill the "Nose" had failed in the past. This attempt succeeded. The murder took place on a Friday at midnight in one of Avena's offices above a gambling and prostitution house. The hit team burst into the room, guns drawn killing four men and John Avena.

It happened fast. As planned, all three of the killers scattered. They were to meet back at the Lanzetta's at two A.M. Biaggio shot Avena in the head. As he turned to leave, he saw a satchel leaning against the desk beside Avena's dead body. Without thinking Biaggio grabbed the satchel, ran down the steps and into the night.

This was Biaggio's first kill, making his bones, and the hit was the head of Philadelphia's largest family. His mind was racing, and he was afraid. As he headed back to his sleeping room to wait until meeting the boys, he lay on his bed staring at the ceiling, trying to calm himself. Eventually, he sat up. Things had been so overwhelming he had forgotten about the satchel. When he opened it, it was full of cash. He knew this was bad, real bad. He wasn't just fearful, he was terrified. He knew enough to understand that if the murder did not lead to a takeover of the Philadelphia Mob, he was a dead man. The money added to his potential problems.

The only thing he could think of was to leave the city immediately. He went to his childhood friend Salvadore Bono's apartment and banged on the door. He and Bono had grown up together. Sally's father owned a small vegetable business and had a truck he used to pick up fresh produce.

Bono opened the door, his eyes half closed. "What the hell are you doing?" He said. "Do you know it's the middle of the night?"

"Sally, I'm in big trouble and need to get out of town now, not tomorrow, NOW!"

"Are you crazy?" Sally said. "Have you been drinking?"

"No man, listen to me. I need to leave Philadelphia right away." He repeated. "I'll pay you if you drive me to Pittsburgh."

"Shut the hell up," Sally said. "You couldn't even buy gas to get to Pittsburgh."

Biaggio pulled a small roll of bills from his pocket, peeled off fifty dollars and gave it to his friend. "Is this enough to get me there?"

"I don't know where you got this, but for a fifty I'll take you to Cleveland."

Thirty minutes later they were in Sally's truck and seven hours after that Sally dropped Biaggio off in an

Italian neighborhood in Pittsburgh. He got out of the truck and hugged Biaggio. "I love you man."

Biaggio said, "You don't know nothing about me, nothing, get it?"

"Yeah, I get it," Sally said. He watched his friend walk away as he got back in his truck. He turned the truck around and drove off. It was the last time either of them saw each other.

After the murder of Avena, a brief open warfare broke out in the Philadelphia Mafia. Joseph Bruno emerged as the boss and put a lifetime contract out on Lanzetta, his brothers, the kill team, which included Biaggio, and their entire families. Bruno was making a statement.

It only took a few days to identify Biaggio. When Bruno's men arrived at Joseph Calegara's apartment, they wanted to know where the boy was. They tortured Joseph and Alessa. When the men were satisfied they knew nothing, they slit their throats.

xxx

Ann arrived home in Waynesburg at ten-thirty, parked her car in the garage and headed into the house. Her husband, Jim, had already gone to bed. She was still keyed up and sat in the recliner on her enclosed porch staring into the darkness. She closed her eyes listening to the night sounds. Her thoughts continued to wander through the story stitched together by her sister Marilyn.

xxx

Biaggio spent a night in Pittsburgh, and the next morning bought a bus ticket for Fairmont, West

Virginia. It was well known in those days that West Virginia was a safe-haven for Mafia family members to cool off when they needed to escape law enforcement. They would disappear from New York, Boston, and Philadelphia to the safety of the Appalachian Mountains into small West Virginia communities. Fairmont was one he had heard of.

As it turned out, he did not go to Fairmont. During the last rest stop in Morgantown, he overheard some men say a local coal mine was hiring. He stayed there, put the stolen money in a local bank under the name Bill Cole. Three years later he left the coal pits, married Sandy Alimento, bought a house and opened a small Italian restaurant. The name and persona of Biaggio Calegaro evaporated into the mists of the West Virginia hills, never to emerge again.

xxx

Ann got up from her chair and went into the bedroom. It had been the conversation with Hank Murdoch that started this. Coffee with him and seeing Mary Cole at the visitation brought all of this back to mind. She changed from her clothes into her nightgown and slipped into bed.

"Everything good?" the sleepy voice of her husband said. "Yeah, hon," she replied. "It's all good."

Drifting to sleep she wondered whether she should tell Hank this story.

CHAPTER 35

Mary was worried when Ann mentioned Hank's name at the funeral home.

"Clayton, I'm in Morgantown. Are you working? I need to talk to you. Can we meet somewhere?"

"What's on your mind?" he asked. She could feel a note of caution and hurt in his voice.

"I went to Gus Cole's visitation at the Hastings Funeral home here," she said. "I spent some time with Ann Stout, his sister-in-law."

"Mary, I don't understand where this is going," Clayton said.

"Last night I had dinner with Hank Murdoch. Today, he had coffee with Ann before the visitation."

"So?"

"We talked about Tony."

Clayton got quiet.

"Clayton. You there?"

"Yes," he said. "Where are you now?"

"I'm just leaving the funeral home."

"Don't come back here, Mary. Do you remember the McDonalds where we used to meet in Osage? Go there and wait. I can be there in twenty minutes."

It took Mary ten minutes to cross the university

campus, through Star City and over the river to Osage. She got a booth by the bathroom away from the counter. Ten minutes after that, Clayton drove into the parking lot.

Clayton wore civilian clothes – blue jeans, a jean jacket and black polo shirt. He was in low-heeled cowboy boots and a dark blue baseball cap with WVU emblazoned in gold letters on the front. Everything he wore had seen better days. He came in the front, quickly spotting her. Before sitting down, he went to the counter and ordered a cup of coffee. During the affair, they met here, leaving one of their cars before going to a motel. Osage was a predominantly African American community. Clayton thought there was less chance of being recognized by anyone they knew.

Clayton walked to her booth and sat across from her. He didn't say anything, and for a few moments just looked at her. There was an African American couple sitting in the booth behind them, and against the window across from them a large black man.

When Anderson didn't say anything, Mary looked down at the table and then glanced out the window. Turning back, she looked him in the eye. "Alright Clayton, I get it, okay? You can turn down the lawman stare and talk to me."

"Good to see you too, Mary," Clayton said sarcastically.

"Look, I'm sorry about the way it ended for us. You have to understand, I just couldn't handle it. I wasn't using you. It just wasn't in me to carry on the way we did. I honestly didn't know how stressful it would be until we were in it."

"Look Mary, I fell for you. Everything about you worked for me. I respected your decision, but I didn't have to like it. I don't like it now. What is going on?"

Mary told Clayton about meeting Hank at Muriale's the night before. She and Hank had dated in high school, and over the years remained friends. When Tony and Susan were murdered, Hank came home to see if he could help Ben.

Mary took a breath, slipping her hand to the back of her neck. She looked at the wall, hoping to find an easy way to say what was coming next. There was none.

"I had a little to drink and Hank made me feel real comfortable," she said feeling her face redden. "Clayton, I told him about our affair."

Clayton's expression went blank for a moment as if he were processing what he had just heard.

"What the hell?" He hissed. His face turned red looking like he was trying to control himself. "What exactly did you tell him?"

Mary felt trapped in the booth. Her heart beat faster and she was short of breath. She had debated whether to mention anything about the threat but knew she had to tell it all.

"The thing is, Clayton, I told Hank you said you would kill Tony if he ever did anything to hurt me."

"Jesus H Christ," Clayton growled. "You told Hank Murdoch that I made a verbal threat against Tony?" His expression darkened. Mary had not seen this look before. She felt his eyes were boring into her soul.

"Let me understand this. I am a deputy sheriff in Marion County investigating the murder of your husband Tony Cole and Ben Miller's wife Susan, for which Ben is our primary suspect. Do you have any idea where something like this could lead?"

"I am so –," Mary started to say.

"Don't say another damn word, Mary. And don't say another damn word to Hank Murdoch. I've got to do some thinking."

The black man against the window got up and walked to the door.

He glanced back through the window at the white couple in the booth. Dequan Terry pulled the phone out of his pocket, got into his car and punched *return call*.

CHAPTER 36

It was just getting dusk when Hank pulled into Bobby Cooper's summer camp in Colfax. He hadn't been there since graduation when John's dad threw a party for the senior football players who had fought gridiron wars together. Hank played sports with John for a good part of his junior high and high school years. Big John's willingness to sacrifice all in the protection of his quarterback and other players created an unbreakable bond of respect and trust between the two.

John was on the front porch swing as Hank came around from the back of the house. "Hey John."

The approaching evening mixed with the gentle sound of flowing water a few feet in front of the building, created a sense of calm. Hank sat in a large wicker chair and put his feet up on the footstool in front of him.

Neither man said anything for a few minutes as they sat in the woods by the river, breathing the cleansing mountain air.

"I love this place," John broke the silence. "Anytime I need to get away and think, I come here. Everything else is unpredictable in the chaotic nature of my life and work, but here? Here nothing changes. It is where I am grounded. This is where I am quiet and find peace."

Listening to John reminded Hank that this behemoth of a man, and the sensitivity of his heart, were a paradox known to few.

"Okay, Hank," Cooper said, "What's on your mind."

Hank told the Sheriff about his dinner with Mary Cole.

"You know I dated her in high school and we went out from time to time when I was on leave. I wanted to see how she was doing and offer any help, if she needed it. We ate at Muriale's. I had forgotten how much I enjoyed that place. After a glass of wine, she opened up about Tony, and the way he treated her. She hated him, and although she didn't know for sure, she felt that if Tony and Susan were having an affair, then they got what they deserved."

Hank watched his friend gently swinging back and forth, staring at the river and listening intently.

"There's more, and this is going to be the tough part for you to hear. Mary had an affair last year." Hank watched John's expression as he gave him the news. "It was with Clayton Anderson."

The swing stopped. John turned his head and Hank felt his friend's eyes drilling through him. "What the hell?" he said. "I don't believe it."

"She told me it began with a possible breaking and entering call out to her house about a year ago. Clayton came to investigate," Hank continued.

"They apparently ran into each other around town. Clayton told her he was sorry Tony treated her the way he did. One thing led to another, and they got into it."

"That's bullshit!" John spat.

Hank wasn't sure whether his comment meant he

didn't accept it, or it was crazy that Anderson would have an affair with a married woman, Mary Cole in particular.

Now that the door was open, there was no turning back. "After a few months, she ended it. Apparently, Clayton reluctantly accepted, but told her if Tony ever did anything to hurt her, he would kill him." Dusk gradually turned to darkness like an invisible curtain drawn slowly across a theater stage, the change barely discernable. They sat saying nothing for a long time. By the time John spoke, he was almost invisible in the darkness. The swing started up again.

"I don't like this, Hank," John said, sounding calmer. "It's a possibility, I'll give you that, but I've known Clayton a long time and it is out of character."

Sensing John was now considering the possibility, Hank told him of his background check of Anderson's military experience. He wasn't sure John knew MP training included tracking and that the standard-issue side arm was a Beretta nine-millimeter.

"Getting a hire who is ready to go on day one doesn't happen very often. Clayton wanted to stay in Fairmont and I was grateful to get him. I have a hard time making him for this. He got out of the Army a year early for family reasons. His mother needed him. He's a good man, Hank."

The two men found themselves in a mental conundrum. Hank believed Ben had nothing to do with the murders and it appeared John felt the same way about his deputy. Hank could also tell that Cooper felt the pressure of having to consider expanding the direction of his thinking. The swing stopped again.

Hank measured his words. "I am not accusing Clayton of anything. I'm just saying one might consider he had the means, his military training, the motive, his feelings for Mary, and possibly the opportunity. It is also conceivable that Mary is involved and put Anderson up to it."

Hank knew what made John Cooper a good cop was his willingness to consider all possibilities without letting his personal feelings interfere.

The men sat a little longer, before Hank closed the loop regarding his day by relating his conversation with Ann Stout.

"There may be an entirely other explanation for these murders. It has to do with something you said to me this morning and why I went to Morgantown. It's the reason I asked whether Gus Cole had an autopsy."

Hank continued, "You said the Monongalia County Sheriff found Gus Cole dead when he went to tell him Tony had been murdered. If they did a post mortem on him, but believed he had died of natural causes, they would collect tissue and blood samples, but not test them further. Why do further testing, right?"

"Shit," he heard John sigh in the darkness.

"I don't know whether they did an autopsy or not. I can check in the morning. It is standard procedure to keep specimens for up to a year. It seems like a long shot, Hank."

By now it was dark. The two of them sat in the dark. The air was filled with the chorus of frogs, crickets, and other nocturnal creatures looking for dinner and a date. The river air had become damp and close.

John broke the silence. "To be honest, Ben was my guy for this. I actually thought this was going to be open and shut, just a matter of finding him and tidying up loose ends. You have given me a lot to think about, man."

"Thanks for taking the time to hear me out," said Hank getting up from the chair.

"One more thing," he said as he turned to leave. "Did your team find anything else at Morris Park?"

"Yeah," Cooper said. "We found a small GPS tracking unit a few feet from the path the perp took heading down the hill. We'll be working on it in the morning. We also followed with Janet Moore. She admitted Susan had asked her to cover for her. Said she had no idea she was going to be with Tony. Janet hated the guy."

Hank was glad to hear about the tracker unit. It let him know he had gained John's trust. Cooper would hold nothing back. The gamble had been worth the risk. It was also good that Janet Moore was off the table.

"Thanks for hearing me out, John." As he began to walk away Cooper said, "If you are into it, would you look at the evidence we have gathered so far? We can't draw attention, but if Clayton is involved in this thing, I would like a different set of eyes on the case. You also need to understand clearly, that if I do this, my ass is on the line. It is totally against policy to let a civilian, and in particular you, be involved in this murder investigation."

"Call me, man. I've got nothing else to occupy my time or my mind." Hank left his friend on the swing. In the darkness, he made his way around the side of the cabin to his car.

As he drove home, Hank felt as though he had tilted the investigation by providing alternatives to Cooper's working theory. On the way, he called Ben and brought him up to date.

"I can't believe John is going to share evidence with you," Ben said.

"Yeah, I think he appreciates the military skill set.

But I'll have to be very careful," Hank said. "With the possibility of his deputy in the mix, he feels he needs an independent set of eyes."

"Maybe," said Ben. "But you can be sure he doesn't think you are independent regarding me. You know he is going to be watching you carefully."

Hank got the irony in Ben's voice.

"I get it," he said. "After I get a look at the evidence, I'll call you back."

Ben didn't respond. "Ben, are you okay?" Hank said.

"Hank, I'm getting an incoming call. I'll get back to you." The line went dead.

Five minutes later, Hank's burner phone rang.

"Ben, what's up? I didn't think anyone had your number but me" Hank said.

"It was Dequan Terry," Ben said. "Guess who he saw just now at the McDonalds in Osage?"

"I have no idea."

"It was Deputy Clayton Anderson and Mary Cole," Ben said

"Now that's interesting," Hank said. "Sounds like things are getting stirred up."

CHAPTER 37

On the drive back to Fairmont, Clayton's mind worked overtime with what he had just learned. He gripped the wheel tightly as his eyes darted back and forth.

What the hell! I can't believe Mary did this. What a mess!

If this got out, her confession would put him at risk.

Hank Murdoch? He knew Murdoch came home to support Ben, but why was he poking around and asking questions regarding the murders? He wasn't a cop.

Clayton didn't know what Hank and the Sheriff had talked about the day before in Cooper's office, but he didn't like the way the two of them seemed to so close. Yes, they were school buddies, but Clayton had grown up in Fairmont, too, and gone to the same schools. It irritated him that the two of them were so comfortable with each other.

Why not me? I've been on the force for five years and seen Cooper every single day. He never acts like a friend. Hell, I still call him Sheriff, even in private.

Then, this morning after meeting Murdoch at the park, the Sheriff sent out the forensic team again. They missed some things during their first pass at the crime scene. That made him look bad and he didn't like it.

Had the son-of-a-bitch said something to the Sheriff? He didn't have any damn authority. Clayton could feel anger welling up inside.

A rabbit scurried across the road in front of him diverting his attention. He swerved and missed it.

Calm. I need to remain calm.

He had never liked Ben Miller or Hank Murdoch. He was happy Miller was the chief suspect in the murders. He didn't let it show, but a warm rush of satisfaction coursed through him when he thought of Ben behind bars – maybe even on death row. It would serve that lucky prick right.

"Hey, Miller," he could hear himself saying to Ben once he was arrested and in jail. "Now what are you going to do? Huh? Army sniper hero? Well, once a killer always a killer, pal."

Yeah, he liked the feeling.

He'd been jealous of Ben since high school. Miller's successes reminded him of his own failures. Ben had been captain of the high school football team, played basketball and run track and field. He was a hero of the Iraq and Afghani conflicts. When he came home, he finished college, got an MBA and a good paying job with the power company. Then he married Susan Gallagher. Clayton didn't pay much attention to their relationship in those days but she was a looker, the stuff of young boy's dreams. Miller had it too easy.

Then there was Hank Murdoch, another prick. He felt the same toward him. Those guys were like the two musketeers in high school. Hank was also a good athlete and well-liked in the community. They were always doing things together. Clayton resented their friendship, because he never had a friend that cared anything about him.

He absented-mindedly opened the car window placing his elbow on the frame.

He continued to burn. He'd been an athlete in high school. Maybe not the best, but he worked hard on the football reserve squad, and gave his best at track and field. Wasn't showing up and working worth something? Those guys were just two more on the list of people and situations that made him feel unworthy and resentful. It had been that way his whole life.

His father left home when he was five. Just when he needed a role model, the man was gone, and never heard from again. His mother worked as a nurse at Fairmont General. She was attractive but lonely. Over the years a number of men, *uncles*, came home with her. Some stayed a while, others were gone like the wind.

Uncles. Yeah, the very thought brought a mixture of anger and shame warming his skin. None of them, not one, gave him any attention. Eventually, they stopped coming, and his mother withdrew into herself.

Two years after Hank and Ben enlisted, Clayton entered the service. He had seen the respect people had for soldiers. He watched online videos of military men and women returning home. He saw how people in Fairmont treated veterans. He wanted that. His intake scores were good enough to become a military cop.

When he finished MP school in Missouri, he was assigned to Fort Rucker, Alabama. Most of the job was routine, but he became a good investigator. He wasn't opposed to using a little force when needed – and sometimes when it wasn't. He liked the deference, and sometimes the fear, G.I.s showed him. It was a feeling of power he had never experienced and that made him feel good. He performed well in the service and was on a twenty-five-year career path. He learned how to do his job and was smart enough to cover himself by shifting blame when he needed to. He saw himself moving through the ranks and becoming a master sergeant someday. The Army was his family with colleagues and friends and meaningful work. He would have stayed for the duration, had his mother not taken ill. When the cancer came, he took an early out from the military to take care of her. He felt she had stolen his world from him and he resented her for this. At least in the service he had a community of respect. In Fairmont, he had nothing.

Nobody said, "Well done, man, that was a great thing to do, Clayton. Not many sons would have left everything to come home and take care of their mother." In his mind, there was nothing heroic about caring for a dying woman. All he got was the task of twenty-four hour care until she was done.

He checked in with the Police and Sheriff Departments for job openings. There were none. In Fairmont, he was once again a nobody, drifting without a rudder.

Then he got a call. A deputy had resigned, and the Sheriff needed to fill the slot. He got the job.

Later, Cooper told Clayton he had noticed his application, but at the time didn't have an opening. When one came open, Cooper jumped on it. He told Anderson that having a trained army cop in the department would make his job easier, be a good fit and a great addition to the force.

Clayton took the job and told Cooper he would not be disappointed. Being a Sheriff Deputy in Marion County and a veteran gave him the respect he always wanted in this community. People talked to him, even admired him. Respect was important to Clayton. Very important.

Clayton was resentful that Hank dated Mary Cole

during high school. Though he had thoughts about Susan and other girls, he had a serious crush on Mary. Every time he saw Hank with her, jealousy welled up inside him. She was two years older, but that was then. Now they were older, two-years difference didn't matter much. After joining the Sheriff's Department, he kept tabs on her. Clayton told himself wasn't stalking her – just keeping an eye out.

Even though Mary had no idea Clayton cared for her, when she married Tony Cole, Anderson believed Tony had stolen something belonging to him. He knew of Cole's reputation with women and had been called out on an occasion when a jealous husband caught Tony with his wife. On one occasion, a betrayed husband tried to kill Tony. Clayton wished he had. He hated Cole.

Later when he and Mary got involved, he thought,

See Cole, she's mine. You got what you deserved. I have her. She chose me!

When Mary ended the relationship, Clayton was crushed. He had tried to convince her things were fine, but she would not change her mind.

"I'm married, Clayton," she said. "Tony doesn't have a problem being with other women, but I can't do this. I thought I could. I was wrong. It just isn't right for me."

Rejected again. This time the hurt was deep and lingering. When she called tonight, he thought maybe she had changed her mind. Perhaps with Tony gone, she wanted to get back together. As it turned out, that was not the case. Worse, now Mary had put him in jeopardy. The pill was doubly bitter.

He pulled into the drive when he got home and parked his truck. He sat for several minutes still holding on to the steering wheel and staring past the headlights into his garage door.

He turned off the engine and reached for the door handle.

"Mary," he shouted into the truck cab. "God damn it!"

He got out of the truck and headed to the back door. If he couldn't have Mary, he was going to double his efforts to see what he could do to dig Ben Miller in a little deeper. He would go to Cooper in the morning, reinforce his belief in Miller's guilt and redouble his efforts to find evidence to build the case.

CHAPTER 38

When Hank got home, Peter and Mags were watching Netflix. His dad paused the show.

His mother got up from the couch, stretched and said. "Honey, it is great having you home for a few days, even though you have been busy. I hope you haven't eaten dinner yet. We decided to wait to eat until you got back. I made your favorite lasagna. It's on the stove."

Mags sighed as Hank put his arms around her. He felt a twinge of guilt for the lack of time he had spent with his folks since arriving home.

"Thanks, Mom," he said. "I'm famished. I smelled it before I even opened the front door. You're the best."

Peter turned off the TV and they all went to the kitchen, picked up the food and headed to the dining room.

"I'm sorry for being so preoccupied," Hank said between bites. "From the moment Ben called me, my brain has been in a mixture of shock and disbelief."

"We know, son," Peter said. "It's been a shock for us too. Neither one of us believes Ben had anything to do with the killings."

"Let's talk about this after we eat," Hank said. The rest of the meal, they caught up on the past five years of

151

each other's lives.

After dinner they returned to the living room. Mags and Peter sat back down on the couch and Hank took an easy chair beside them.

Mags piped in. "You got in after dinner with Mary Cole last night, went to the computer and then left so quickly this morning, we didn't get a chance to talk about the case. Have you learned anything you can talk about?"

Hank felt he needed to say something about what he had learned. He wasn't sure how much detail to give them. He decided to keep it on Mary and his dinner conversation with her. He wouldn't tell them about working with John Cooper or that he was in contact with Ben.

"I feel sorry for Mary," he began. "She really suffered from Tony's fooling around. Not only could he not keep his hands off other women, but he didn't seem to care that Mary or anyone else knew about it."

"It was a real scandal at the college with Sally Jenkins," Peter said, referring to President's wife. "I'm on the university counsel. Some of the members felt we might have to ask Rick to step down from the presidency. There was no way to keep it contained, after an investigative reporter for the Times-West Virginian posted photos on their site. There were two clear shots of Tony and Sally going into and out of the Super 8 in Morgantown. They were kissing in a third picture. The Super 8 for God's sake! Rick was so angry and humiliated, he said his first instinct was to kill the bastard."

Peter's comment caught Hank's attention. He had considered the possibility of Jenkins' involvement in the killings, but in light of Mary and Clayton Anderson, he hadn't thought much about it. Maybe he should rethink it.

"Do you think it's possible Rick might have been behind this, Dad?"

"Mother of God, he's an academic, son, not a killer," Peter replied.

"I get that Dad, but you know better than most, people's actions are not always predictable," Hank said. "Betrayal and public humiliation can be powerful forces."

"I'll give you that it's a possibility, but from my personal and professional point of view, it is pretty remote," Peter said.

Hank paused for a moment gathering his thoughts, and turning the page "Let me catch you up on what I've learned."

When he finished recounting the evening with Mary, Mags asked, "Do you think it might have been Clayton Anderson, or maybe he and Mary?"

"I'm not sure," Hank replied.

His parents had a few more questions, but Hank begged off, saying he was tired. He reminded them everything he shared was confidential and circumstantial at best. He hugged and kissed them both then went to bed.

A lot had gone on since the his dinner with Mary the evening before. He had seen Cooper, met with Ben, and had coffee with Ann Stout. Most interesting was Dequan Terry's call to Ben. There were now even more unanswered questions. As he lay in bed, he wondered what was coming next.

He spent the night tossing and turning. Morning took a long time to come, and when it did, he wondered what unexpected thing the day would bring.

CHAPTER 39

After Hank left, John Cooper sat on the porch of his summer camp staring into the darkness. He had a lot to think about. Thirty minutes later, he pulled his phone out and hit speed-dial for his father's funeral home.

"John," Bobby said recognizing the number. "What's going on son?"

"Dad, these murders are getting more complicated. I'm out at the camp. Hank Murdoch was here earlier and has given me a lot to think about. I need to talk to you."

"Come on by."

Even though the hour was late, Bobby was at the mortuary finishing up an elderly woman who unexpetedly died of a stroke. The prep room is not a place most people see. It is not exactly a morgue, but it's antiseptic with the sweet, sickening smell of preservative chemicals. Its appearance was a stark contrast to the viewing rooms where friends and family went through the ritual of saying goodbye. Bobby Cooper was in the business of bringing a sense of closure for them.

John didn't think of his father's profession as one of merely preparing bodies and helping people in their time of grief. Bobby was a warm and compassionate man, but it was a business and a part of John's DNA. For him coming to the funeral parlor wasn't a place of the dead, it was just coming home.

When he arrived, Bobby hugged him and said, "Let's go to the office and sit awhile. Tell me what's on your mind."

John and his father were close. They talked about everything. Maybe it wasn't protocol for the father to tell personal stories he learned from families of the dead, nor was it right for the son to talk about cases he was working on, but there were no secrets between them. This was comforting, providing a sense of safety and complete trust. They felt a release in sharing one another's burdens.

"I don't get it, Dad," John started in. "My first thought when I got to the scene was that Ben might have done this."

"Why did you think that?" his dad asked.

"It was the way the bodies were shot. Both were hit twice. The entry wounds were tightly grouped. Tony's head was almost taken off with what appeared to be a single knife stroke. The murders had all the signs of professional killings. You ask me why? Ben was an army ranger and sniper. Even though his work was for our military, he was trained as an expert killer. He and Hank spent their time in the war tracking and eliminating bad guys. When they were home on leave they talked to me about some of the missions they had undertaken. Their job was to do whatever it took to eliminate enemy threats. Granted, most of the targets were taken out at distance, but they did close up work too."

John saw Bobby look away and stare at the wall with blank eyes.

"Yeah," Bobby said quietly, "I worked on Tony

after his body was released from the morgue. That neck thing was pretty gruesome. I was glad Mary decided to cremate him. It would have been hard to make him look normal in a casket."

In his mind's eye, John saw Tony on the table, pale and lifeless, with the gaping wound in his neck.

Bobby broke the silence. "You have known Ben since you were in grade school. Do you really think he could have done this?"

"I didn't want to," John replied, "but my job is to step away and ask the questions. When I began that process Ben ended up in the crosshairs. It is circumstantial, I'll grant you that, but he fit the profile. There's that PTSD thing too."

"To be honest, I never really understood PTSD," Bobby said. "But I heard Ben had some problems and got counseling after he came back to school. I think Hank's father got him some help at the VA Hospital in Morgantown."

"Dad, you know some of the cases I've talked to you about? The things I see as Sheriff? Just like my work, soldiers are exposed to life in ways normal people don't understand. Everyone needs some kind of outlet. If it weren't for being able to talk to you, I would probably suffer from PTSD too."

"I hadn't thought of it that way," Bobby said.

"Here was another part of my reasoning," John said.

He went on to recount Tony Cole's public attentions to Susan Miller. She had flirted with boys and men as long as he could remember. These tendencies were just as evident when she came back to Fairmont. He told Bobby about the tumultuous, on-again, off-again, relationship with Ben during those years.

"Ben was hooked from the start, but never seemed

to fully come to grips with her behavior toward other men. Jealousy, Dad, it can eat a man alive."

"God knows I've seen this sort of thing tear families apart," Bobby said.

"So, Ben was pretty much the focus of my thinking," John said. "Until I met with Hank tonight at the river."

John recounted the dinner that Hank had with Mary Cole the night before, and the anger and shame she felt at Tony's skirt chasing.

"Here is where this whole thing gets crazy and has blown my mind. Mary Cole confessed to Hank she'd had an affair with my deputy, Clayton Anderson. Not only did this go on for some time, Hank said she told him Anderson had made a threat against Tony's life."

"The thing is," John continued. "At the moment, it's only hearsay, but the deputy has the background and training to have pulled something like this off. He was also the first on the scene. So now, in addition to what might come to light in the coming days, I have two primary suspects."

Bobby had been listening to John work through his attention to Ben. When his son brought up the deputy possibility, he looked like he had been caught off guard.

"You said this looked like a professional killing, and that Ben has been joined by Clay Anderson as possible guilty parties." Bobby said as though he were processing the information.

As often happened with Bobby Cooper, he took some time saying nothing. John had gotten used to this and waited his father out. When Bobby started talking again, John wasn't sure where he was going.

"You know, son, it's hard to believe that something like this could happen here. But that was not always the case. There was a time when a lot of dangerous men lived in Fairmont. If you and I were having this conversation in the 1920s, it might not have been so unreasonable to think a professional killing could have happened."

John was confused. His dad seemed to be going off on a tangent.

"In those days," Bobby continued, "the *Black Hand*, a part of the Mafia operated freely in these parts. They were connected with a broader network in Chicago, Cleveland and east coast cities like New York and Philadelphia. People were extorted, homes and business dynamited, and a number of people murdered. It is said contracts were ordered, not just for an individual, but for their entire families and children. They would stay open until everyone was dead. No matter how long it took."

John looked up at his father.

What the hell is he talking about?

CHAPTER 40

There wasn't much Bobby Cooper didn't know about Marion County. Maybe it was because of the hundreds of stories he had heard from families whose loved ones he had buried. Maybe it was because of Dora Grace Emerick, a woman he had known since childhood. *Dora G*, as folks called her, was Director of the Marion County Historical Society. She was smart as a whip and knew more about the county than anyone.

The funeral home was downtown, and during the spring through the fall, Bobby and *Dora G* could be seen at a small table on the front porch of her building, sharing tidbits of the County's rich heritage.

Bobby was aware of the stories of gangsters coming to Fairmont in the 1920s and 1930s to hide from the law. There was an underground railroad, where members of the mob came to Pittsburgh from New York or Philadelphia. From there, they traveled into small towns in West Virginia. When things cooled off, most of them returned. For some crimes, the men could never go back, so they stayed. Many that remained, married and formed strong Italian communities. Fairmont was one of those places. It was from these men immigrating to West Virginia that the *Black Hand* emerged.

"I had forgotten those stories," John said, remembering his father's penchant for telling tales of Marion County's history. "But what's the point?"

Bobby said, "I'm not saying this has anything to do with the murders of Tony and Susan, but for the sake of argument, what if it did."

Even though John couldn't see it, he began to understand why Bobby had taken the conversation in this direction.

"It seems a little far-fetched," he said. "But I'll keep it in mind."

He had come to appreciate his father had a way of looking at things from entirely different perspectives and directions. He usually didn't understand at first, but had a habit of revisiting them, because Bobby was often right.

Struggling with a decision related to his earlier conversation with Hank, John glanced around his father's familiar office. Turning back to Bobby, looking he said, "You know I'm pretty damn good at this job, but I feel like this is bigger than I thought. I need your advice on something."

"I'm listening."

John replayed a brief timeline. "Hank got a call from Ben early Friday morning and flew here from California on Saturday. By the time he got here, Ben had disappeared. Not a good sign."

Bobby nodded and said, "Go ahead, son."

"In addition to having dinner with Mary where she spilled her guts, Hank had poked around the crime scene the next day. The forensic team had wrapped things up the morning before and removed the tape. He found evidence that my team missed along the tree line. It was pretty embarrassing."

John went on to tell his father what Hank discovered and that he was impressed by what a good tracker and thinker the man was. It was Hank that dug out the potential alternative suspects in Mary and his deputy.

"I know this is against protocol, but I asked him if I could share evidence with him privately," John said with some discomfort.

"You already asked him, so what do you want from me?" Bobby asked.

"I want to get your feelings about it," John answered.

"You know this could be a problem," Bobby said.

"Yeah, if I get caught, it could make matters much worse for Ben, and might even cost me my job."

"Do you trust Hank?"

"I do," he replied, "In some ways more than people in my own department."

"If that's your feeling, son, I would suggest you show him photographic evidence, but do not allow him in the evidence room to see or touch anything. If anyone saw him there, it would be a problem and make things much worse."

John looked at his father, appreciating the wisdom and counsel this man had. Cooper had sworn to uphold justice and the Constitution of the United States. He also knew that the law, as important as it was in civil society, sometimes needed to turn a blind eye.

He was about to look away.

CHAPTER 41

Wednesday, June 18th

Hank was up early Wednesday morning. After breakfast, he grabbed a cup of coffee before walking over to Ben's porch. It was the perfect place to think through everything he had learned. Most interesting was Dequan's call to Ben. Was there a conspiracy between Clayton and Mary? Anderson called in the murders. Had he killed them and then notified Cooper? Had this been a crime of passion on his part? Hank's attention began to focus on Anderson. He was going to spend more time checking out the Marion County Deputy Sheriff.

He ran through the case for an hour and then headed to the gym on campus. He had access because his father was on the faculty. He hadn't exercised since his last boot camp in San Diego Friday morning. He had a need to free his mind, sweat and punish himself. An hour later, as he was leaving the field house, he got a call.

"Hi, Hank, this is Alice in your Dad's office."

"Hi, Alice. Are you new?" he asked. "I thought Marybeth took care of Dad."

"I'm a temp," she replied. "Marybeth has been out

with a cold. She'll be back tomorrow. An older gentleman came by a few minutes ago and dropped off a manila envelope for you. I asked his name, but he said to say you would understand when you looked inside."

Five minutes later Hank climbed the steps to his father's second-floor office in Hardway Hall. He thanked Alice for the envelope and walked next door to the student union. Grabbing a large soft drink, he chose a table in the corner of the cafeteria and opened the envelope. Inside were evidence photographs from the murders of Tony and Susan. Hank glanced around to make sure nobody was close by.

The pictures were graphic and reminiscent of what he had seen when serving overseas. Camera flashes lit the night pictures. They were stark and surreal. The morning shots clearly showed where the shell casing and footprints were found. The next pictures, he knew were out of sequence, but showed the place the killer left the site, the GPS unit and dried footprints on Pleasant Valley Road.

The GPS tracker was small, the kind that could be purchased online. There was a serial number along with a manufacturer's code that identified when and where it was made. It might be traceable.

It was when he got to the photos of the shell casing that he sat up as though he had been jolted with a Taser. They were blown up and taken from different angles. On one side of the casing was a small mark. To the untrained eye, it would have meant nothing. Without context, not even the most astute forensic detective would have paid attention. But if you were an Army Ranger and a sniper, the mark was like a mega sign on Broadway in Times Square.

"HOLY SHIT!" Hank hissed out loud. "The son of a bitch was one of us!"

Looking around, he realized some of the students at other tables were looking at him. He caught the eye of a coed, smiled, put the photographs back in the envelope, left the building, and jogged back to his house. At his rental car, he opened the glove box, pulled out the disposable phone. His mind was racing.

He hit the speed dial. Two rings in, Ben's voice said, "Yeah?"

"Ben, you are not going to believe this," Hank blurted out, his heart pounding. "Forget Clayton and Mary. I think I might know who killed Tony and Susan."

"Slow down, man, what are you talking about?" Ben said.

"A half-hour ago, I got a call from my Dad's secretary. She said an old guy left me an envelope at his office. I think it was probably Bobby Cooper. I went to the office, picked it up and stopped by the student union to check it out."

Hank told Ben everything he saw from the photographs. He saved the shell casing for last.

"Do you remember that guy we trained with who was compulsive about marking his kill rounds?"

"You mean that guy from Pennsylvania, who always talked about how much he loved to hunt with his dad? The guy who couldn't wait to deploy because he wanted to kill bigger game?" Ben asked.

"Yeah, that's him. The one who said he was glad the military would allow him to get some of that Haji meat."

"That guy always bothered me," Ben replied. "I wondered how someone like that got by the psych screening."

"Wasn't he on a four-man sniper team? I remember we ran into him in Kandahar during our second tour."

"Yeah," Ben said. "What the hell was his name?"

"Dooley, maybe. Doolittle?. Dudley? It was 'Do…' something. Yeah, I think it was Dooley," Hank said

"No, that's not right," Ben said. "Give me a minute.'

The phone went silent. The only thing Hank could hear was the pounding of his own heart and his breath.

"It was Delaney," Ben said sounding sure. "Mark Delaney…."

"You're right, it was Delaney," Hank said, as though the man's image came clearly to his mind.

"What the hell does it mean?"

CHAPTER 42

Hank agreed to talk to Cooper about this development. "Before I call him, you and I need a face-to-face. I'll meet you at the same place as yesterday. By the way, don't eat lunch, I'm bringing food," he told Ben.

Hank smiled. They had consumed a lot of military MREs in their day. He thought Ben might enjoy something a little more appetizing than the prepackaged food he had been eating.

Forty-five minutes later, Hank parked his car in the pullout near Cooper's Rock, got out of the vehicle, whistled and waited. He heard Ben's return signal from the direction of the small clearing where they met the day before. Grabbing the sack with biscuits, scrambled eggs, bacon and two cups of black coffee from the passenger's seat, he walked into the woods toward the clearing.

Hank entered the opening, but didn't see anything. Then he noticed a small mound ten feet into the tree line to his right. Ben had created a nest.

"Not bad," Hank said in a loud voice. "It looks like you've still got it, but I think my grandmother would have seen you if given an extra minute or two."

Hank heard his friend laugh out loud as he emerged from his nearly invisible hiding spot. "Your grandmother and a small team of rangers," he replied.

They embraced and then sat on the ground against a couple of trees. It was still, with only a gentle breeze. It was quiet on the ground, the leaves acting like baffles in a sound proof room.

Hank knew Ben was still coming to grips with his loss, but felt that if he could keep his friend's mind engaged with the investigation, it would help.

"I can't believe this," Hank began as Ben dove into the breakfast food. "Why would Delaney want to kill Tony and Susan? I thought about it all the way up here."

"I have the same question," Ben said, "but now I'm pretty sure Susan's murder was not part of the plan. I have no idea what the plan was, but I think Tony was the target."

"After your call last night, Anderson looked really good for this," Hank said. "I thought about him this morning and on my way to the gym. I had begun to put together a case."

"I thought so too," said Ben, looking up at the open sky in the small clearing. "We still don't know enough to completely rule him out, but I'm liking Delaney. I just don't have any idea how or why."

"I agree," Hank said, running his fingers through his hair. "We need a plan." Ben nodded. "Yeah, we should pull things together."

Hank pulled a notepad from his shirt pocket and began to write as he and Ben reviewed everything they had on the case.

"Here's what we know," Hank reviewed the notes. "For some reason, Tony and Susan were at Morris Park on Thursday evening. We don't know why. Somewhere between eight and nine, they were murdered."

"Cooper came to my house at midnight to give me the news. I thought Susan was out with her girlfriend, Janet Moore. I was stunned. After John left, I realized I might be a prime suspect."

"Yeah, I get it," Hank said, returning to the things they knew about the crime scene. "They found boot prints both at the scene and the next day on Pleasant Valley Road that appeared to be military and matched your size."

Ben interjected, reviewing what they knew, "You told me only one nine-millimeter shell casing was found. The shooter must have policed the brass, but got interrupted and didn't have time to get it all. The car coming up the drive scared him off. He must have used a silencer, because the kids in the car didn't hear anything. We believe now, from the marking on that shell casing, it belonged to John Delaney."

"To that point," Hank said. "The double shots to the left sides of their heads, indicates that Delaney must have slipped up from behind the driver's side of the car and surprised them. The slitting of Tony's throat suggests he was the main target."

Ben took a deep breath, sighed and winced as he looked across the small clearing. Hank knew he was running a scenario through his mind and could feel his best friend's reaction.

"Sorry, Hank," Ben said. "I flashed on Susan on that slab in the morgue. And I can't help feeling guilty that she must still be there. I should be home organizing her funeral, not on the run as the prime suspect in her murder!"

Hank moved over to Ben, put his arm around his friend's shoulders, gave him a quick hug, then leaned back. "Man, I can only imagine," he said in a quiet voice. He hated that this is what had brought his best friend and him back together.

"I think it would be good for us to stay focused, Ben. You and I know you did not do this. The sooner we sort it out, the better it will be."

Hank appreciated that what he said, was less important than being supportive. He also knew that staying on task was the best thing he and Ben could do.

"Okay then," Hank continued. "Delaney, who we believe killed them, headed back to his car through the woods. The markings on the trail suggest he fell, dropping a portable GPS he was carrying. We can surmise this is how he tracked Tony to the park. We also found fresh tire tracks next to the Valley Lounge, where Delaney likely parked his vehicle."

"It looks like we can rule out the affair Mary Cole had with Clayton Anderson and the threats he made against Tony. The same goes for Rick Jenkins for being humiliated by his wife's behavior," Ben said.

"There are a couple of loose ends we don't have answers for yet," Hank said. "We don't know whether the death of Tony's father, Gus, on the same night has any connection. Until forensics returns the rifling data, we don't know exactly what kind of weapon was used. Most of all, we have no idea what Delaney's motive was."

The good news was that Cooper had not yet put out an all-points bulletin for Ben. Hank and Ben knew that unless something happened quickly, the Sheriff would do just that, making things much more challenging.

There was work to be done, and it was clear that Ben needed to be an active part of it.

"How secure is your camp?" Hank asked. "I mean,

can you safely leave it for a couple of days?"

"If I need to leave, I'll just take my things with me," Ben said.

"For the next step, it would be better to not have your gear with you."

"I can bury and camouflage it. What do you have in mind?"

Hank detailed his thinking. "I'll contact Cooper to see if there is any news on the Gus Cole autopsy. I'll try to get an update on the FBI forensics lab. Maybe the rifling results will be in from the bullet that killed Susan." He would also see what the Sheriff was doing regarding his deputy Clayton Anderson.

"You need to get to a library with computers to do some background work on Delaney. You could get on the floor of my backseat, and I could drive you someplace like Uniontown. Do you have any civilian clothes?"

Ben smiled. "Don't worry about me, man. When we get done here, you go back to Fairmont. I'll get to Uniontown and get some clothes, no problem."

Hank checked the location of the library there and the closest hotel on his iPhone. Ben wrote the information down. The next hour was spent working on their plans for the following twenty-four hours, then Hank left.

When he was gone, Ben took out his phone and dialed a number.

"Yeah," said the voice on the other end.

"It's Ben. I need another favor."

CHAPTER 43

On his way back to Fairmont, Hank called John Cooper. He got his voicemail.

"John, Hank here. I was following up to see if you had gotten anything back from the FBI lab on the slug, or the autopsy on Gus Cole. Give me a call when you get this and, by the way, thanks for the package you left at Dad's office."

There wasn't much else he could do until he heard from John. From the time he arrived home from California, he had been actively moving forward with this case. While he wasn't licensed to do private detective work in West Virginia, his criminal justice training and military skills had served him well. A lot had been accomplished in the past few days.

He was sure he had made the break in the case, but knew he couldn't reveal it to Cooper. It would be better to wait. He hated to wait.

He was on the outskirts of town when his phone rang.

"Hank, John here."

"Hey, John, any news?"

"Nothing yet, Hank, but I plan to call them right after lunch. By the way, it was Dad who dropped off the package with some of the things we talked about. Did you get a chance to look at it?"

Hank knew he wasn't going to say anything about what he learned from the shell casing photographs.

"Yeah, I did look at them briefly. I'll check them in more detail when I get home tonight. I want to make sure they remain secure," Hank replied in a matter of fact tone. "Any news on the autopsy?"

"As a matter of fact, yes," Cooper said. "There were traces of potassium chloride in Gus Cole's system. The coroner examined Gus again more closely this morning and found two needle marks on his neck. It looks like this is murder."

"Man," Hank exclaimed. "I could just feel their deaths the same night were not a fluke."

"One more thing, Hank. That GPS device had no prints, but did have a recorder chip in it. Whoever killed Tony and Susan, planted it on Thursday morning in the gym parking lot on campus. This was confirmed by university surveillance video. They put it up last year for coed safety and protection against vandalism and theft. A man dressed in a polo shirt and khakis, can be seen walking toward Tony Cole's SUV. He looked around, then bent down, and appeared to put something in the driver's side rear wheel well. Unfortunately, he was wearing a baseball cap and we couldn't get a look at his face. We know he was Caucasian and we estimate his height at six-feet. By the way, we traced the GPS. It was bought at a tech store for cash. It's a dead end."

"This is a lot of information. Does this change your thoughts about Ben?"

"Maybe, Hank," said Cooper. "But it sure as hell would've helped if Ben hadn't run off and disappeared."

"Yeah," Hank said. "That would be helpful,

wouldn't it?"

CHAPTER 44

After a restless night thinking about Mary, Clayton showered and headed for work. Whatever fleeting thoughts he had that she wanted to get back together evaporated like the early morning mist.

After the shift briefing, he stopped by the dispatch desk. "Brad, would you let the Sheriff know I would like to see him sometime today."

"The Sheriff beat you to it, Clay. He left a note for you to stop by his office over your lunch hour."

What the hell is this about?

He glanced at Cooper's office. The door was open. He wasn't there. The Sheriff hardly ever asked for an individual meeting with his Deputies. Usually, if there was something on his mind, he'd pull them aside to let them know what he was thinking. Being called to his office was not standard procedure for his boss.

Clayton was scheduled for patrol, but changed assignments with Deputy Jenkins, who had rotated to desk duty that morning. Aside from the receptionist, the office was empty. He sat alone at the desk. Glancing around the room, he adjusted his chair, turned on the computer and went to work on Ben Miller.

Clayton wasn't going to leave a stone unturned. He did the usual background checks through the standard law enforcement databases. The Department of Motor Vehicles, warrant, and local police records turned up nothing of any significance. He worked through screens providing Ben's social security number including physical description and body markings. Not much there. He accessed federal and state criminal history databases but found nothing.

Feeling mild frustration, he got up from the desk and walked to the coffee pot. He poured a cup, leaned against the wall and stared out the window. His mind clicked. He had an idea.

Despite Clayton's feelings for Mary, he had not been without female companionship since returning to Fairmont. The first year back, he met Charlene DeLuca when he investigated a minor fender bender as she turned off the highway into her driveway. The driver behind her was on the phone and not paying attention. Her car was struck a glancing blow on the driver's side rear bumper.

At the scene, Clayton calmed the two drivers down. Nobody was hurt, and insurance would cover damages. He took their names, contact information and gave the man a warning about cell phones and cars. Clayton could tell the girl liked him.

A few weeks later, after the case cleared, he followed up with her. Charlene was a nurse's aide at the hospital where his mother worked before her cancer got bad. She told Clayton she had made the connection right away. They dated for several months, but eventually realized it was not a good fit.

His crazy hours and her constant fear for his safety were more than she had expected. It sounded like an excuse, but Clayton was okay with it. He had been feeling bored with the relationship anyway. The separation was friendly.

He made the call. "Char, Clayton here. How are you doing?" he began. After some small talk, he told her he needed a favor.

One of the things Charlene liked during their relationship, was getting inside information that was not available to the public. It made her feel important and in the know.

People in her line of work are practically invisible in the health care system. They move freely and overhear confidential conversations between doctors and nurses all the time. While they were dating, she talked openly to Clayton about the information she got. It was like they were co-conspirators sharing things they should not be telling one another.

Charlene was a floater. She worked on different floors and in various hospital departments. This meant she spent time in the mental health unit. She was on that unit part of the time when Ben Miller had been initially evaluated for PTSD. She recognized him but said nothing. From bits and pieces of conversation, she learned he had killed a lot of people in the military and needed help to work through it. He had been sent to the University Hospital in Morgantown for further evaluation and counseling. This was one of the things she shared with Clayton. At the time, it was mildly interesting but meant nothing to him. That was then.

"Char," he said. "I'm investigating the murders at the reservoir Thursday night. What I'm about to tell you is highly confidential. Can I count on you?"

Every time he told her something and said it was highly confidential, the tone of her voice would lower and sound conspiratorial.

"What is it you need to know, Clayton? I don't know anything about the murders."

"Do you remember when you told me about Ben Miller's evaluation at the hospital for PTSD?" he asked.

"Yes," the sound of her voice showing increased interest.

"Look," he continued. "We have not charged anyone in the killings yet, but Miller has disappeared, and I'm just checking around to see –"

"Clayton, I don't have any idea where Ben Miller is," she said, interrupting him.

He sighed. Interjecting before he got out what he wanted to say was one of the things that irritated him when they were together.

"No," Clayton, said patiently. "I want to know if you can quietly poke around to see whether there is more information regarding his PTSD evaluation."

"Gee, Clayton, I don't know. All that stuff would be in his electronic medical record. The system logs everyone that accesses patient information," she said. But he could tell by the tone of her voice she was curious. Charlene was clever and understood the hospital records system. If anyone could get a look at Ben's records, without being noticed, it would be her.

She paused, "So are you thinking Ben was the killer?" her soft voice getting a little higher.

"I don't know, Charlene. Just let me know if you find anything that might suggest Ben had violence issues."

"I'll let you know if I find anything. And Clayton, I've kind of missed you." She hung up. A mild tingle moved through his body and his face flushed. For a moment, he considered calling her after all this was over.

"Clayton, in my office," the Sheriff's voice interrupted his thoughts.

CHAPTER 45

Clayton pushed back from his desk and walked across the room to Cooper's office.

"Close the door and take a seat, Deputy."

Deputy? Something isn't right. The tone of the Sheriff's voice was firm, too firm.

"What's up Sheriff?" he asked, feeling uncomfortable.

"We have a problem," he said, looking directly at Clayton, his eyes focused and unwavering. "And, at the moment, you are it."

Clayton immediately braced for the onslaught.

He broke eye contact, glanced out the window and then back to his boss. He rubbed his trousers with his hands.

"I'm not sure what you mean, Sheriff," he said.

"I will make this brief. A couple of years ago, you had a burglary call at the Cole home. Is that correct?" Cooper asked.

"I did," Anderson replied, attempting to sound calm.

"Subsequently, did you enter into a relationship with Mrs. Cole?"

"I, uh, ran into her –," he sputtered.

"Deputy," Cooper interrupted, "I'm not asking for a story, I'm asking you a direct question. Yes or no?"

Clayton's face flushed and his mouth got dry. He took a deep breath and let it out before answering. "Yes sir, I did."

"This is pretty damn disappointing," the Sheriff said. "You know there is a policy against this sort of thing. It may not be against the law, but we have a higher standard. Do you realize the effect on our Department if this became public knowledge?"

"Yeah, to be honest, I just didn't think about it at the time," he answered shifting his gaze to the window again. "It was poor judgement on my part."

Clayton's mind was on fire.

What exactly did Cooper know? Did Mary call him out of a guilty conscience? Did Murdoch tell him what Mary said to him at their dinner? Did he know about the threat? Shit!

Cooper sat quietly for a moment, not lifting his gaze.

"Now's your chance, Deputy," he said. "We have two murders on our hands. I need to know you are not implicated in any way. I want to know everything."

When Clayton came in that morning, he intended to find as much as he could on Miller, go to Cooper and continue building the case. He thought the idea to call Charlene was a stroke of genius. Now he realized it could be a terrible mistake. If Cooper shifted attention to him, the Charlene connection would eventually come out. Everything had changed, and he knew hiding information would be fruitless. At that moment, he realized if he held anything back, it could mean the loss of his job, and maybe his career.

"After the burglary call," Clayton began, "I saw

Mary around town a few times."

He told the whole story. How the affair began. Where they met for the two months they were together. He wanted Mary to divorce Tony, but she wouldn't do it.

"She's the one who broke it off," he said. "To be honest, I wanted to keep seeing her."

Cooper's expression had not changed during the confession.

"Is there anything else you want to tell me?"

The air was charged. Clayton made a decision.

"Yeah, there is," he said, his voice lowering. "I told Mary if Tony hurt her, I would kill him."

"You did what?"

Clayton extended his hands, palms facing forward, as if trying to stop the question. He raised his voice. "The man disgraced her time and time again. He was a pig with no conscience. I cared about her. When she broke it off, I'll admit it, I was hurt bad. It just came out."

"Take a breath and settle down Deputy," the Sheriff said gruffly. "We have a problem here. For all of us, not just you."

Despite the seriousness of the situation, Clayton sensed a subtle shift in tone from an interrogation to a leader looking to protect his own.

"Anderson, you know this is not going to end here, but it's enough for the moment. I need to do some thinking. At least, you were honest about the affair. Is there anything else you want to tell me?"

"No," Clayton said feeling like his whole world was about to come crashing down around him. His face was drained of color and he looked down at the floor.

"Alright then, go back to work, and shut the door

on your way out."

When Clayton was gone, Cooper got up, walked around this desk and pulled the window shade down on the door. He needed some privacy to think things through.

Returning to his chair, he pulled a ruler out of his drawer, leaned back and put his boots on the desk. Tapping his thigh with the flat edge, he absent-mindedly glanced around the office and out the window. He saw nothing as his mind processed everything he learned over the past two days.

The information Hank had given him about Mary and Anderson the night before was startling.

His decision to confront his Deputy about the affair was the first step. He had come to trust Anderson. He was a good cop with the right instincts. This thing with Mary Cole and its potential link to the murders was not good, but at least the man had come clean.

Cooper sat up and reached for his phone. He called the FBI in Clarksburg. "Agent Priester," came a voice on the other end.

"Jim, John Cooper here. I'm calling about the slug and casing I sent you. I know you just got them Friday, but I thought I'd take a chance and see if you had any luck so far?"

"As a matter of fact, I have," said Priester. "We just got it done. Give me a minute and I'll pull up the report."

Cooper heard the agent pecking on his keyboard.

"The rifling indicates it came from a Beretta PX4," Priester said. "Does that help you out John?"

"I'm not exactly sure, Jim, but it'll narrow things down. Email me the report, will you?"

Priester said he would, and the two men hung up.

Cooper put the phone down. He knew Deputy Anderson's personal weapon was a PX4. He swiveled the chair putting himself in front of his computer screen and looked up gun registrations in Marion County. Ben Miller also owned a PX4.

His next call was to the courthouse. A woman's voice said, "Judge Spencer's office."

"Judy, Sheriff Cooper. Is the Judge in?"

"Judge Spencer," a voice came on the line.

"Your Honor," he said. "I need a search warrant for Ben Miller's place. I'm looking for a weapon that might have been used in the murders last week of Tony Cole and Susan Miller. I have evidence that it was a Berretta PX4. Ben owns one of these."

After giving him the details, Spencer said he could have it ready in fifteen minutes. Cooper hit the end button and picked up his portable radio.

"Serdich, this is the Sheriff. Call me on your cell phone." He didn't want his conversation overheard by anyone. His cell buzzed.

"Sheriff? Serdich here," the Deputy said.

Cooper told him to go by Judge Spencer's office, pick up a search warrant and meet him at Ben Miller's place.

"Deputy, keep this to yourself. Do you understand."

Serdich said yes. Thirty minutes later he pulled into Ben Miller's driveway. The Sheriff was waiting.

xxx

By now the office was busy with officers coming in and out filing reports and booking suspects.

Back at his desk, Clayton sat down. His shoulders

slumped. He was drained. After a few moments, his mind re-engaged.

Holy shit! I need to stop Charlene and call her off.

He picked up the phone and dialed her number. "Hi, this is Charlene. I can't come to the phone right now. Leave a message."

"Char, this is Clay. Call me as soon as you get this. It's important."

xxx

Charlene DeLuca was in her supervisor's office when the cellphone buzzed in her uniform trouser pocket. Slipping it out, she glanced at the screen. It read *Clayton.*

She was sitting in front of Mr. Alampi's desk because she had been caught accessing unauthorized patient information using a vacationing doctor's password.

Charlene had enough to worry about. She let the call go to voicemail.

CHAPTER 46

Security found Charlene on the third-floor general medicine wing sitting behind a computer terminal. She was confronted and escorted to the hospital's head of safety, William Alampi. He was a small man with thinning gray hair, and beady brown, unblinking eyes. He was not given to many words, and had a reputation as a stickler for protocol.

Sitting in front of this man, Charlene was afraid. The air conditioning in his office made the room chilly and added to her discomfort.

Alampi got right to it.

"Ms. Deluca, I need to know why you were attempting to use Dr. Toothman's User ID and Password?" he asked.

The Electronic Medical Record system had been upgraded earlier in the week. One of the new security features, activated access to appropriate employees and doctors when they swiped their badges at the hospital entrances. If someone tried to access their account without swiping their badge, even with the correct User ID and Password, it would be denied. A silent alarm would then trigger and identify the terminal where an attempt was being made. The medical staff had been made aware of the changes.

Charlene knew denying what she had done could lead to a possible arrest and federal prosecution for violating patient information protection laws. She was also cunning and had to come up with something fast.

She looked the man directly in the eye.

"Mr. Alampi I did try to access the hospital database with Dr. Toothman's ID and Password," she said. "I knew it was wrong. Forty minutes ago, Nurse Kettering, the supervisor on the surgery floor, paged and asked me to get a report on an appendectomy patient, Mr. Lawson."

This was true. She had been asked for the report, but had gotten distracted by Clayton's call and the system timed out.

"I forgot to print the report and was afraid a double query into the patient's file would raise suspicions," she said. "I don't want to get Dr. Toothman into trouble, but I've pulled information for him in the past and knew his user ID information. I was aware he was on vacation. When I tried, I couldn't get in the system. I thought I had mistyped the password, and was entering it again when I was caught."

Alampi listened to her story. He shuffled some papers on his desk, cleared his throat and said. "Ms. Deluca, you are a good employee and have been here a very long time. You know, I could fire you on the spot."

"Mr. Alampi, I –" she interrupted.

"I am not finished, young lady," he said. "I am going to speak with your supervisor about this, but recommend you receive a written warning to be placed in your file. Do you understand?"

"Yes, sir I do," she replied. "Thank you for not firing me. I give you my word this will never happen again."

"I hope not," he said. "Now report to your supervisor. You are dismissed."

Eva Brown, Charlene's supervisor, was waiting for her with a stern lecture about how she could not only have been fired but possibly arrested. Charlene apologized all over herself, telling Nurse Brown it would never happen again.

She knew it was a close call. But there had been enough truth to her story, and her apparent open confession had done the trick. The important thing was that she didn't lose her job. Equally important, she was going to have a conversation with Clayton Anderson.

xxx

Clayton answered her call on the first ring.

"Char, am I ever –"

"Don't say a word, Clayton Anderson," Charlene exclaimed before he could finish. "I almost lost my damn job this morning because of you. As it is, I got a verbal and written warning."

He could tell by the tone of her voice she was livid. She related every detail of what happened from the time he called her. It came out fast and as it did, she began to calm down.

"Did you say anything about me?" he asked hesitantly.

"No I did not, Mr. Deputy Sheriff," she replied. "I was too busy trying to cover my ass! Alampi and my supervisor said I could have gotten arrested and gone to jail."

A wave of relief swept over Clayton. He knew better than to say much, so he kept quiet as she continued.

"I've done this a hundred times before, but Alampi told me they just put something new into the computer systems as a security double check. I'm telling you, Clay, that man scared the shit out of me. At first, he just sat there staring before he said anything. I felt like a damn fly in a spider web."

Usually Clayton smiled when Charlene swore, because it only happened when she was upset or scared. At the moment, his expression was cold stone serious. He was thinking she wouldn't have been the only one who could have been arrested and gone to jail.

After she had gotten most of it out, she said, "I gotta admit, Clay, it was pretty damn exciting when it started. The first time I put in the password and stuff, it didn't work. I thought I had messed up. I just redid the password again when the security guard showed up. Man, I freaked out. I got sent home, but it coulda been worse. I'm pretty relieved." She paused and her voice softened, "Listen, maybe we could get together on the weekend."

Clayton took a breath convincing himself he probably needed to do this.

"I'll call you tonight," he said. "I gotta get back to work."

He hung up the phone.

"Shit!" he grumbled under his breath.

CHAPTER 47

Cooper was leaning against the Department SUV when Deputy Serdich got out of his patrol car. The Sheriff had purposely not involved the forensic team. Deputy Anderson was the forensics lead, but Serdich was the second best he had. If they found anything that required further investigation, he would call his people in. Cooper knew his own limitations.

"You got the warrant?"

"Right here," Serdich said as he unbuttoned his shirt and pulled out the white envelope. The Sheriff removed the document and gave it a quick look.

"All right, let's get to work. I am going to take the house, you look in the barn. If we're careful, we can be done in an hour. If you find anything, let me know right away."

Cooper went up the porch steps and paused in front of the door. Putting on a pair of latex gloves, he turned the knob. It was unlocked. Once inside, he stopped and visually swept the living room. Nothing stood out. Then he noticed Ben's phone on the island kitchen counter dividing the two rooms. He made a note and went into the kitchen.

The sink was empty. A coffee pot, cup, silverware and a plate were in the drainer. He opened the cabinets, refrigerator, and oven – nothing unusual.

Ben's small office was neat with everything appearing to be in its place. He sat in Ben's roller chair, turned on the computer and waited for it to fire up. It was password protected. Cooper looked through the drawers on the desk to see if it was written down anywhere – nothing.

He got up and worked his way through the bookcase. On the top shelf facing the desk was a wedding picture of Ben and Susan. The couple looked happy. That Susan had been a real looker. Despite her well-known behavior, John was one of the few who genuinely liked the woman.

What a shame.

Next was the bedroom. The bed was crisply made and had a wooden chest at its foot. He opened it. It was half full of camouflage clothing and not much else.

Ben might have taken some things when he disappeared.

The walk-in closet had two sets of clothes – men's and women's. Above both sides of the wardrobe were cabinet doors. Cooper started on Susan's side. Shoes and sweaters and boxes filled the shelves – nothing remarkable. On Ben's side, he found sweatshirts, a computer hard drive, and some connecting cables. On the top shelf of the second cabinet were shoeboxes. He pulled them down. The bottom two held a pair of old running flats and dress shoes. The top box got his attention. It was empty, except for a two-year-old Walmart receipt for a couple of disposable phones. The Sheriff pulled out his smart phone, took their pictures and replaced the boxes.

Cooper returned to the living room, mentally processing what he had found.

"Sheriff," Serdich's voice shouted from the bottom

of the porch steps. "I think you're gonna want to see this."

When Cooper came out of the house, Serdich said, "Come with me to the barn."

"There wasn't anything unusual down here," his Deputy said glancing around the inside of the building. "But check out what I found up there." He pointed to the loft.

They climbed the ladder. "Over here," he pointed. "I found this cabinet. The damn thing is locked, but you can see dust has been disturbed like someone opened it, took stuff out and laid it on the ground," Serdich said, pointing at the area around it.

Cooper saw the lock had a combination and key mechanism.

"Get your pick kit, Deputy. Let's take a look inside."

Joe Serdich was a good forensics officer, but when it came to getting into locked cars, houses or buildings, he was the best Cooper had ever seen.

The Deputy returned with his tools straightaway.

When the cabinet doors swung open, Serdich whistled. "Man, check that out. There's all kind of military gear in there."

What was not there is what got Cooper's attention. The left side of the cabinet was packed with a flak jacket, rations, military rifle, sighting scope, and a hand gun. It was neatly arranged. It looked like there should have been two full sets, but the right side of the cabinet with the exception of a pistol, was mostly empty.

Cooper knew Ben and Hank had rifles and PX4 Berettas. They registered them when they moved back to Fairmont. When they first returned from the military, they practiced at a long-gun range near Clarksburg.

Mindful of possible PTSD issues with returning combat veterans, Sheriffs in the adjacent four county area informally kept each other up-to-date regarding who was using these target ranges. It was just a precaution. As time moved on, Hank and Ben visited the range less and less. John couldn't remember the last time he heard Ben had been there.

"Deputy," Cooper said "it looks to me like Ben Miller has taken his gear and gone to ground somewhere." Cooper took a picture of the open cabinet and told Serdich to lock it back up.

"What do you want to do about this, Boss?" Serdich asked when he was done.

"Joe," he said, glancing around the loft. "Other than the Judge, nobody knows we were here, and I want to keep it that way for now. Clear?"

"Yes, sir."

The men returned to their vehicles and drove back to town.

xxx

Cooper tried to think as though he were Ben but realized it was fruitless. Miller had evaded hunters trying to kill him in their own countries. Obviously, they had not been successful. If Ben wanted to stay a ghost, there wasn't much Cooper could do about it.

Maybe I can't find Ben, but I can damn sure get hold of Hank. Friends or not, Hank had better not be holding out on me.

He took his phone and made the call. It went to voicemail.

"Hank, where the hell is Ben?"

CHAPTER 48

By the time Dequan picked Ben up and drove him to Uniontown, it was two in the afternoon.

On the way, Dequan asked, "What are we looking for when we get there?"

"I need to get to the public library and find a place to stay for the night," Ben replied.

When they got to Uniontown, Dequan drove past the library on Jefferson. Within a couple of blocks, there were several small hotel and motels. On West Main, Ben saw the Highland House Hotel. "Drive past the place and drop me off." Ben said.

Dequan dropped him off at the corner. Taking his things out of the back seat of the car, he reached in and shook the big man's hand. "I might need to call you again, once I'm done here," Ben said.

"Call me if you need me. I'll come and get you," Dequan said.

Then with a broad smile he continued, "You knows, though, I has got to take care of my reputation. Too many folks keep seein' me with a boy as white as you, and they gonna be talkin'." They laughed out loud as Dequan drove away.

Ben threw his knapsack over his shoulder, walked

back to the Highland House and checked in. He gave a fake name to the clerk.

On their way into town, Ben had written down the license number of a car in front of them. He put this and the make of the car on the hotel registration form. He knew nobody would check.

"How much is the room?" he asked the woman behind the desk.

"It's fifty dollars a night," she replied. He paid for two nights in cash.

"Thank you, Mr. Rochester," she said as she looked over the registration form and handed him his magnetic card.

"Is there a drug store nearby?" asked Ben.

"Yes, there's two. Walgreens and CVS, both within a couple of blocks," she said giving him directions. He thanked her, dropped his knapsack in the room and walked to the CVS.

He picked up some personal items, a couple of Pittsburgh Pirate tee-shirts, and a Steeler baseball cap. Then it was back to the hotel. The first thing he did when he got in the room was strip off his clothes, take a hot shower, brush his teeth and lie down for thirty minutes. The bed felt good.

He knew he needed to try and rest, but was excited that he and Hank were on the hunt again. They were a team again. He wasn't sure where any of this would go, but getting out of the nest and becoming an active part of this made him feel good. As he lay on the bed, his mind drifted to the first assignment he and Hank had been given in Iraq.

xxx

It was Iraq in 2002, and it became clear this job was deadly serious. Their first Haji hunt was for Rukan Razuki Abd al-Ghafar who headed the Iraqi office of Tribal Affairs, nicknamed the RAG. He was the *Nine of Spades* on the most wanted list of the American Military Command. Intel had him moving from the outskirts of Bagdad to Tikrit in the early morning hours. Their intel indicated he would be meeting a boat on the northeast side of a small island in the Tigris River, where he would depart for Bajii. The kill opportunity was the watercraft rendezvous.

They set their nest across the river at midnight and waited. As the grayness of the day began, a small boat moved in from the north. It pulled up to the shore across the river from Hank and Ben. Thirty minutes later four men on foot came into view.

"Target." Hank whispered to Ben as he identified 'the RAG.'

"Standby,' he continued, concentrating on his breathing.

"Roger," replied Ben, sighting on the target.

"Range three hundred fifty meters."

"Roger and ready," Ben said quietly.

"Take the shot," whispered Hank, keeping his attention on the man.

"Shit," Ben heard Hank curse under his breath.

Just as Ben sent the round, the RAG turned to someone behind him. A split second later, a head exploded into a pink mist, but it was a man standing beside him that took the round. It was a miss.

Hank was supposed to have said, "Send it," but in the excitement, neither one of them noticed it. "Take the shot" seemed natural and stuck becoming their 'code' for the rest of the time they hunted the most dangerous animals of all – men who were their enemies.

xxx

Ben brought himself back to the present in the hotel. His skin was coated with light sweat, his breath fast and heart rate faster. He sat up and swung his feet to the floor. Resting his elbows on his knees he covered his face with his hands. Taking a few deep calming breaths, he got up, slipped on one of the new tee-shirts, jeans, boots, baseball cap and headed out the door for the library.

CHAPTER 49

The Library was a large redbrick building with a modern art sculpture just outside the main entrance.

"May I help you?" asked a plumpish lady sitting behind the desk just inside the library door.

"Can you tell me where your public computers are?"

"They're at the top of the stairs to the left. If they're full, put your name on the wait list and take your turn."

Upstairs, the computer room was busy with people staring at and clicking through the screens that had their attention. Three of the computers were unoccupied.

He sat down in one of the empty chairs, clicked the browser button, and opened Google. He searched for his Ranger School graduation class photo from April 2002. He quickly found Hank and himself sitting on the second row. It took him a couple of minutes to locate Delaney.

Gotcha, you son of a bitch.

Delaney was in the seventh row, the sixth man from the right. He hit the print button and walked over to the printer. After retrieving the photo, he circled Delaney's picture and continued his search.

After an hour of digging and finding nothing, he thought he might give Scotty Hardesty a call. Scotty went through Ranger and Sniper Training with Hank and him at Fort Benning. He had four years with a couple of tours under his belt before separating to Washington, D.C. where he had grown up. After undergraduate school at Morehouse College in Atlanta, then attended Georgetown University Law School and returned to Washington to join the Department of Veteran's Affairs in 2012. He and Ben kept contact for a while, but life moved on, and by 2014, they lost touch.

Ben wasn't sure where to start. He searched for the Office of General Counsel in the Veterans Affairs website, and found a link to a list of legal service clinics, but there weren't any staff names available. Each state had contact information to include addresses, kinds of services provided and when the offices were open. He thought he would start with the District of Columbia and printed the contact information.

When he was back at the hotel, he asked the girl at the front desk whether the hotel had fax services.

Smiling, she said, "Yes, and the first three pages are free. After that it's fifty-cents a page."

He thanked her, went to his room and called the General Counsel's office in Washington, where he spoke with the attorney on call. The woman had never heard of Hardesty, but suggested he call Walter Reed and gave Ben the number.

"Walter Reed National Military Medical Center," the operator answered.

"May I have the legal services department, please," Ben said.

The operator put him through. A man answered. Ben explained that he understood this was a long shot, but there was an attorney with Veterans Affairs with whom he had served in the military, who he was trying to track down.

"Just a minute," the voice on the other end said, and Ben was put on hold.

"Colonel Watson," a gruff sounding voice broke the silence. "I understand you are looking for an attorney by the name of Scott Hardesty."

"Yes, sir," Ben replied

"Who are you and what do you want with Mr. Hardesty?"

Ben explained he was an ex-Army sniper who had served four tours in Iraq and Afghanistan, and that he and Hardesty had served together. He said he was thinking about coming out to the Washington area in the next few months and wanted to track Hardesty down to catch up on old times. Watson asked him a few questions related to where he had served and with what divisions. Ben felt like the old man was giving him a verbal lie detector test.

"You're in luck, son," the Colonel said. "I might be able to help you. I don't know exactly where Mr. Hardesty is located, but he came through here a couple of years ago after graduating from law school. He was an excellent and dedicated young man."

"Yes, sir," Ben replied. "I didn't get much from the GC's office."

"I can understand why they didn't help you when you called them earlier. They're pretty careful down there about giving much information."

Let me give you a different number at the agency. It's a direct line to Lionel Williams, chief counsel there. Tell him Tom Watson gave you his number. Tell him he can call me if he needs to. Good luck, young man. I know the work you did was unacknowledged, but I want to personally thank you for your service." Ben wrote down the number, thanked him, and disconnected.

Within an hour, after talking to Commander Williams, a familiar voice answered the call, "Hello. This is Scott Hardesty."

"Scotty, it's Ben Miller, how the hell are you?"

"Ben Miller. I'll be damned. I'm great, thanks. How are you doing?"

Ben had thought about how much he should tell Hardesty, but considering the evidence Hank had uncovered, he decided to be forthcoming.

"Scotty, I've got a problem."

Ben brought Scotty up to date on the murders and his decision to go to ground.

"Man, I am so sorry to hear about your wife," he said.

"Thanks, Scotty, I'm still in shock about the whole thing. Hank came in from California last Saturday. Monday, he met with the Sheriff, and with tacit approval began a parallel investigation of the murders."

Ben told Hardesty how Hank had found a couple of potential suspects, with motive, means, and opportunity. In the end, though, it was the local Sheriff's trust in Hank that led to this call.

"Hank was unofficially given access to photographs of the forensic evidence and noticed subtle markings on the shell casing. He recognized them as from one of us. Do you remember Mark Delaney?"

"Delaney? What a prick. I never liked that guy," Hardesty said. "You think he killed your wife and brother-in-law? Why would he do that?"

"I do think it was him. I have no idea why he did it. I want to track him down without drawing attention."

"I don't know what I can do, man, but let me check

around."

Ben explained he wanted to see Delaney's personnel records. They were availble but the official request needed to be vetted and would take ten days. That was too long.

"Say no more, Ben. One of the advantages of being an attorney in the DVA, is that I can look at records online. Give me an hour and I'll call you back."

An hour and fifteen minutes later, Ben's phone rang.

"Ben, Scotty here. I'm not sure what this means. The records indicate Delaney was killed while on assignment in Afghanistan in 2009. Was Hank sure about this?"

"Hank was absolutely confident the markings were the same ones Delaney used," Ben replied.

"This might be a little trickier because of our computer logging system here, but I know a guy at the Pentagon who might be able to dig a little deeper. Give me until tomorrow morning."

"Thanks, Scotty," Ben said.

"No guarantees, man. I'll call you tomorrow."

CHAPTER 50

On his way home, Hank's mind was still trying to sort things out. He stopped at Palatine Park in Fairmont and let his mind wander as he sat by the river.

He was lost in thought when his cell buzzed. He looked at the screen. It was John Cooper. He wasn't sure why, but warning bells rang in his mind. He let the call go to voicemail. The military had sharpened his instinct, and at the moment the alarms were saying something wasn't right.

After hearing John's brief message and his tone of voice, Hank knew he was right not to answer. Not knowing what John wanted exactly, he got up and walked around giving some thought before returning the call.

Fifteen minutes later Hank he made the call. He was prepared for whatever might come.

Cooper answered his phone sounding tired and irritated. He got right to it. "Hank, I want to know where Ben is, and don't give me a bullshit answer. I'm not in the mood. I just came back from searching Ben's place. I found a receipt for a couple of disposable phones and a half-empty locker cabinet where, apparently, you guys store military gear. I'm pretty damn sure Ben took his stuff out."

Hank said nothing. "I feel like you have been playing me, man," Cooper sounded like he was trying to control himself. "I don't like it one bit. The FBI report came in, and the weapon used in the murders was a Berretta PX4. I know Ben has one, and I think it was in that damn cabinet."

Hank still said nothing.

"Well, where is he?" Cooper questioned tersely.

Hank knew it took a lot for John to blow his top. He also knew when the threshold got crossed John Cooper could be a force of nature. The man sounded like he was right on the edge. He wasn't going to lie to John, but he also wasn't going to be entirely forthcoming.

"You're right," Hank said. "I have been in touch with Ben. I should have told you right away, but wanted to do some background work before I did. I thought it would distract from the investigation I was doing. It was never my intent to keep anything from you, there were just some things that needed sorting out. I'm sorry I didn't tell you, okay? But the truth is, I don't know where he is. He said he was going to prove he didn't kill Tony or Susan and that he had some leads he was going to follow."

"And the cabinet?" Cooper said forcefully.

"Look, John," Hank began. "I haven't seen the locker for years. Yeah, we both stored gear in it, but I have no idea what might be missing. There could be things I don't –"

"What was supposed to be in it?" Cooper interrupted.

Hank knew this was not a time to fool with his old friend. "We each had weapons – handguns and rifles.

There were flak vests, backpacks. I had a spotting scope. Other than that, some MREs and small tactical gear are about all I can remember."

Hank could feel Cooper coming down from the mountain.

"Jesus Christ, Hank," John said sounding disgusted. "Listen to me and listen to me good. You get in touch with Ben Miller ASAP and tell him to get his ass into my office. Do you understand me? And by the way, you are now on a very short leash with me. I trusted you, gave you evidence that I should not have. If I wasn't exposed for having done that, I would arrest you and throw you in jail for impeding this investigation. Do you understand me?"

"I understand you completely," Hank replied in a steady voice. "I'll try, but I honestly can't guarantee I can get him in. Give me a day."

"You have until Friday morning, and I don't give a damn if I get into trouble myself, I will come after you. Trust me that this is the last thing you want. I am deadly serious about this." The phone went dead.

xxx

Hank called Ben. He answered sounding animated. "Man, I was getting ready to call you. I just got off the phone with Scott Hardesty. You remember he trained with us in sniper school and did some hunting tours. After separating, he became a lawyer and is working for the Veteran's Administration. He has access to personnel records and does searches all the time."

Ben brought Hank up to speed on what he had learned, including, unfortunately, the information that Delaney had been killed in the war.

Hardesty was going to look a little deeper but would have to go through back channels to see if he could find any more detail. Ben was on a roll. Hank waited until he was done.

"So, we may have to reconsider who the killer might be," Ben said after getting it all out. "What do you think?"

"I really don't know," Hank said at the disappointing news. "But right now, we have a bigger problem."

He related his conversation with Cooper. "John knows we're using the burner phones. I didn't admit anything, but he knows. He wants you in his office Friday morning. It was an ultimatum, not a suggestion. He sounded as pissed as I have known him to be. I'm pretty sure if you don't come in, I'm going to be arrested for obstructing the police investigation, and then we're dead in the water."

Ben was quiet for a few moments, then said, "I have to think about this, man. I hate to put you at risk like this, but I need to think. We've made significant progress on the murders. If I come in, we might both be arrested."

"I'm prepared to let the chips fall," Hank said. "If I have to go to jail, I will, but it will make it a lot harder. If you get found, we're done."

"Yeah, I get it," Ben said. "I need to go for a walk and get some fresh air. Scotty said he would call me tomorrow. I'll get to you asap, and we can decide what we should do." They hung up.

When the call started with Ben, Hank felt upbeat, but at the news of Delaney's death, he didn't know what to think. He took a deep breath as he looked across the river to Fairmont's downtown. Cloud cover blocked the sun, the air didn't feel fresh anymore, and things looked like they were going to hell.

CHAPTER 51

Thursday, June 19th

Ben was up most of the night worrying that the work he and Hank had done might have been for nothing. The Delaney news had been a blow, and he wasn't sure what to do next.

He guessed he could pursue the Anderson lead. What did Gus Cole's death mean? Was it unrelated? He couldn't make anything work. If he came in, what would that lead to? There were too many questions, and he couldn't see a path forward.

The hell with this.

He went for a run, ate breakfast and waited. At ten o'clock, Ben's phone rang.

It was Scotty. "Ben, I have some news. It looks like Delaney is still alive and kicking after all. You remember we wondered how a guy like that could have gotten through the personality screening? Well, they let him through purposely to watch him. In '09, he was recruited for black ops – wet work. He had no family, so they fabricated his death to take him off the grid and created a new identity. He separated from the military, with the new name, in 2012 and was picked up by the

CIA for special assignments. He goes by the name of Arthur Eberhard, but he may work under different aliases."

"Why the hell would the CIA want to kill my wife and brother-in-law? Does anyone know where he is?" Ben asked.

"I doubt the CIA had anything to do with this. My source believes he lives in Philadelphia and moonlights as a free-agent for the Mafia and others. He is apparently discrete and damn good at what he does."

Ben's heart began to race. "Scotty, I don't know how to thank you for this."

"We've seen a lot of shit, more than we should have," Hardesty said. "But no one can take away the brotherhood. Let me know if you need anything else."

Hardesty hung up, and Ben immediately made a call.

"Hank, I just got off the phone with Scotty. Delaney is alive." He brought Hank up to date on Delaney's status, including where he lived and the alias he was using.

"I have no doubt Delaney committed all three murders."

"Yeah," Hank said. "I still don't see a connection. I wondered—"

"Let me finish," Ben said. "When Scotty said Delaney sometimes did work for the Mafia, pieces began to fall into place. I remembered you told me Ann Stout said Gus's father talked about a mob killing when he was young. You said he was afraid the mafia would track him down, killing him and his family."

"Ann thought it was just the dementia talking," Hank said.

"Yes, but what if it wasn't just an old man's ranting? What if it was true? What if Tony and Gus were part of a revenge mob killing, and Susan was collateral damage? What if Delaney took the contract and tracked Gus and Tony down?"

"You could be right," Hank replied, "But how would we prove it?"

"We don't need to prove anything. You and I can work on that later. From what you have told me, the forensic evidence will clear me, Clayton Anderson, Mary Cole and the College President, if he was even a serious suspect."

"You're right," Hank said

"I gave your conversation with Cooper a lot of thought, Hank, and even before Scotty's call, I decided to come in. I left because I wanted to find Susan's killer. With your help, I think we've done that. As far as I can tell, the evidence against me is circumstantial. I can't see that there will be a problem."

"You will need to come in and bring your Beretta for John's team to test," Hank said.

"Not a problem, man," Ben said pushing the disconnect button.

Then he made one last call. "Dequan, I need one more favor."

That night, a blue Mustang convertible pulled into a driveway on Route 250 just north of Fairmont. A figure wearing a Pittsburgh Steelers baseball cap got out of the car, grabbed a fully loaded backpack from the back seat and shook hands with the driver.

Ben Miller was home!

CHAPTER 52

The next morning at six, Hank walked to Ben's house, climbed the steps, opened the door and yelled, "Hey big boy, you up?" Ben came out of the bedroom barefoot, wearing a tee shirt and a pair of shorts. It looked like it had been a rough night.

"Good to see you home where you belong," Hank said, hugging his old friend.

"Yeah," said Ben, "Come on in the kitchen. I'll put on some Java."

After making the coffee along with some bacon, toast, and eggs, they headed to the porch. Like old times, they took a couple of chairs and sat at the table. The past few days had been traumatic.

"So, how's your head?" Hank said after they settled in and began eating.

"I don't know man," Ben said. "All of this has happened so fast. It's only been a week since Susan was killed. My mind is still spinning. I expected to wake up and find this was a nightmare. I mean, Jesus, I lay awake in the nest at Cheat Lake every night trying to make sense of it. I thought getting home would help. Last night wasn't much better."

Hank knew he needed to let Ben talk. He sat in

silence.

"What the hell was she doing with Tony at Morris Park? I still don't get that. I know they liked each other, but she was like that with a lot of guys we knew. She was just wired that way. As far as I know, it was always just talk. I never believed she would cheat on me. Then there is Mark Delaney. I want to kill the bastard, and I want to find out who hired him."

Hank said, "Let's hang until a little later this morning then go see Cooper. As soon as he checks your Berretta, he will know it wasn't you for sure. Maybe he even has more information."

"Yeah," said Ben, "but I don't want to give up Delaney. He belongs to us. We need to hunt the son-of-a-bitch and put him down."

"Agreed," Hank replied.

They spent the next couple of hours shooting the breeze as Ben talked about finishing school, the PTSD counseling, and marriage to Susan.

"In the beginning, it didn't take much to trigger an episode," Ben said. "But your dad and the VA at the university helped me through a pretty dark time. There is no way for people to understand the things we did. The program in Morgantown had Vets on staff. They knew…they knew."

"That was a good thing," Hank said.

"I know you, and a lot of people, thought Susan was a bitch," Ben continued running his fingers through his hair. "But she was like an addiction for me. There were parts of her nobody understood, not even me. She was a mystery, Hank, but I loved her "

Both men stared over the valley.

Ben broke the silence. "We've been so busy with the case, I haven't even asked what happened after you left school. When you came in for the wedding there was no time either. What have you been doing since you left school and Fairmont?"

"School wasn't working. I guess I wasn't able to adjust to civilian life. I only passed one class that fall. How the hell does that even happen," Hank said with a smile. "I mean, who fails at Fairmont State? So, I headed out and drifted. I thought a change of scenery would help. I knew you were struggling and thought hanging around together wouldn't be good for either one of us."

Ben gave a knowing look and said, "Yeah but you know there was a lot of support here."

"You know how much dad wanted me to be successful. I just didn't care about anything, and facing him every day was just too much."

"Your dad really helped me through a pretty rough patch, but I can understand it's different when it is your father," Ben said. "So what happened next?"

"I ended up in California but kept moving up Highway One. I stopped in Cannon Beach, Oregon, met a girl and hung with her for a couple of months. It didn't work out, so I went to Portland. It rained like hell there, which by the way matched my mood exactly. Then it was San Diego – still in a haze."

Hank told him about the Criminal Justice course at Miramar College and the military private eye work he had done. He talked about the Ranger Boot Camp exercise programs. Most of his time was chasing small time offenders and girls from his exercise class.

"I was passing time man, just passing time." Hank stopped for a moment as a smile crossed his face. "I've gotta say though, working with you this past week is the best thing I've done since heading west five years ago.

Damn, I've missed this."

Since they were kids, Hank and Ben had an easy way between them. They weren't kids anymore and had seen and done things few would ever know or understand. What counted was that *they understood.* They got quiet for a long time.

"I don't know what to do, Hank," Ben said finally, breaking the calm as he gazed straight ahead with unfocused eyes. "I don't know how to feel. I'm tired and angry and confused and want to hurt somebody bad."

"I don't know either," Hank said staring into space. "The only thing I know to do is what we did during the war when things were tough – put our heads down and take the next step."

Hank was in a trance as the valley below became a blur of browns and greens. When he looked over at Ben, he saw tears trickling down the sides of his face. He got up, patted his old friend on the shoulder and said as he headed down the steps, "We'll go to Cooper together and get this done. I'll pick you up at nine o'clock. And Ben, bring your Berretta."

CHAPTER 53

When they arrived at the Sheriff's office, the waiting room was empty. Hank sat down as Ben went to the window and asked to see the Sheriff.

"Tell him, Ben Miller is here."

In a couple of minutes, the door opened, and Cooper appeared. It was evident he was not happy. "Ben, where the hell have you been? Come in." Hank got up as Ben started through the door.

"Sit back down, Hank, I want to see Ben alone," he said. Hank stopped and looked at Cooper with surprise. The waiting room door closed and he went back to his seat.

Cooper led Ben into his office and shut the door. He was angry with Ben for disappearing. Friend or not, he wasn't going to sugar coat anything.

"You know, man, I'm pretty pissed about this. I'm tired, I'm angry, and I feel like you've been jerking me around."

"Look, John, –"

"Damn it, Ben, it's about trust, and your account with me is pretty low right now. In the beginning, I couldn't believe you could have done the killing, but you flat out disappeared. That and how professional the

murders appeared, made you look like the chief suspect.
"

"Yeah," Ben agreed. "I know how it looked. To be honest, I didn't care. I needed to find out who killed Susan and thought if you arrested me I wouldn't be able to do anything."

Cooper gave him a stern look and didn't say anything for a few moments.

"Tell me everything, after I came to your house last Thursday night. I mean everything," Cooper said.

Ben glanced around the office, his eyes flat and distant-looking, as if he were reliving the night. He took a deep breath.

"At first, I was in complete shock," he said. "I couldn't believe Susan was dead. After you left, I was awake most of the night."

Cooper watched Ben's face and eyes as he spoke, looking for telltale sign that he was lying. He knew subterfuge was part of Miller's training, but the Sheriff had a keen eye cultivated through years of interviewing talented liars. Even though he had come in, Ben was still his only serious suspect. He dismissed Anderson as a possibility when the Deputy came clean about the affair with Mary Cole.

Ben described his thought process for Cooper and detailed the timeline once he decided to leave Fairmont. He told him about hitchhiking north toward Morgantown and then to Cheat Lake State Park where he camped out until coming in this morning. He did not mention Dequan.

"Tell me about Hank's involvement," John said.

"Early last Friday morning I called him in California. He said he would be home by Saturday evening. I knew it was possible I would be the chief suspect and decided I couldn't take the risk of being brought in. So I made the decision to leave early Saturday morning, and was gone by the time he came to town."

"I hadn't thought everything through, when I left. I was camped in the woods, and after the first night, I realized I couldn't do much without help. I texted him on Monday to let him know I was okay and gave coordinates for a place to meet. I gave him a burner phone when I saw him."

Cooper was impressed that Ben was so forthcoming. Hank had been very helpful at the murder scene, but now he understood it wasn't until Ben and Hank were working together that the bigger picture began to emerge. While he still was not convinced Ben was innocent, he had to admit these two were a formidable team.

When the Sheriff felt like he had gotten the background information he needed, he said, "Ben, I need your handgun." He had been focusing on Ben like a bird of prey the whole time during their conversation. He paused and said, "Ben Miller, I'm arresting you on suspicion of the murders of Tony Cole and Susan Miller." Cooper read him his rights.

"What the hell," Ben said with a shocked look on his face. "I don't understand, I've told you everything from our last Thursday until right now."

"I get it," John replied. "But, I need to run your handgun through forensics and, to be honest, even though I think I believe you, I am not taking the risk that you will disappear again."

"Disappear again?" Ben questioned, his voice getting louder.

Something was happening to Ben. He looked

defensive, and his eyes moved rapidly around the room.

"It's for your own good," John said.

"My own good? My own good? Christ," Ben said. "You're wanting to put me in a cell?"

"I'm going to hold you until the forensics are back on your weapon."

"You don't need to lock me up, John," Ben said his speech more rapid. "I'm not going anywhere."

Cooper saw fear in Ben's eyes for the first time.

"You're not going anywhere because I'm holding you until I get this cleared up.'"

Ben started pacing back and forth, then shouted in Cooper's face, "Damn it, John, I'm not going to jail. Do you understand me?"

Now it was Cooper who was shocked. He had never seen Ben like this. He looked like a man on the edge, about to come completely unglued.

The Sheriff was a much bigger man, but he didn't want this situation to get away from him. By now Ben's eyes were glazed and wild-looking. He began breathing heavily with a mist of sweat on his forehead. There wasn't time for John to get help.

He stepped back from Ben, planted his feet and in a loud and firm voice, "Soldier, look at me."

Ben was still pacing.

"God damn it, soldier, I said look at me!" he shouted.

As if something clicked in Ben's mind he stopped and looked at John. It was like Cooper's voice brought his mind back to the office. Their eyes locked. Ben's breathing slowed.

"Sit down, Ben," Cooper said, quietly. "Sit down."

As Ben sat down, looking at the floor, the color

drained from his face.

Cooper was shaking inside. He didn't want to think about what might have happened had Ben lost control. Cooper was sure, without help, Ben could have hurt him badly – maybe killed him. He took a deep breath to calm himself. His desk phone rang. He listened and said, "No, I'm not finished. Tell him I'll come get him in a few minutes."

When Cooper hung up the phone, Ben said in a low voice, "The gun is in Hank's glovebox."

CHAPTER 54

Hank didn't like the tone of John Cooper's voice when he took Ben back. He particularly didn't like it when he was told to sit down and wait. It was too formal. Something was wrong.

Twenty minutes later, Hank went to the window. "Can you check with the Sheriff and see how much longer he'll be?"

The woman made the call. "He said it will be a few more minutes."

By now the voice in Hank's head began to yell at him. Cooper opened the door and said in a serious and official tone, "Hank, come on in."

Hank got up and went through the door to John's office. Ben was not there.

"Where is Ben?" Hank asked.

"Close the door, Hank."

When the door was shut, Cooper continued. "I've arrested Ben on suspicion for the murders of Tony and his Susan. May I have the keys to your car?"

"What the hell are you talking about, John? Arrested him? The keys to my car? Why?" Hank was shocked.

"Ben said his Beretta is in your glove compartment. Give me the keys and I'll send one of the Deputies out to get it."

"This isn't right, John," Hank growled, a flash of rage exploding inside.

"It's procedure, Hank. I can hold him for ninety-six hours on suspicion of murder. Ben is a proven flight risk and my primary suspect. We have to get ballistics on his weapon. I'm going to keep him in custody until I'm confident he is clear."

Hank could not believe Cooper. He struggled to keep control. "Have you checked Clayton Anderson's weapon?" he questioned, still in utter disbelief.

"I am not going to discuss the case any further," Cooper said.

"Not discuss…not discuss?" Hank hissed, trying to contain his building anger. He could feel his face flush.

"John, we shared evidence with each other," Hank continued doing all he could to keep from shouting. "And you know without my help, this investigation would have gone nowhere. I brought Ben in for Christ's sake."

"Look, Hank, I'm not taking the chance that Ben will run. I'm damn sure not going to take the chance of losing him again. He is not going to go anywhere until I get forensics on his gun."

"This is bullshit, John!" Hank said, fuming.

"The sooner you give me your keys, and get Ben's weapon, the sooner I can move forward."

"Can I at least see him?" Hank asked defiantly.

"He's in booking. Once that's done, and I've got him safely behind bars, you can see him for fifteen minutes. I'm doing this by the book, Hank. If you have a problem with that, deal with it." He held out his hand. "Now, the keys?"

Hank was incredulous. He gave them to the Sheriff.

He could not believe this was happening.

xxx

Clayton Anderson was in the office when the Sheriff and Hank had words. He stopped in to drop off some citations and wasn't sure of all that went on. But when the men came out of the Chief's office, neither of them looked happy. He knew Cooper's expression and was glad he was not Hank Murdoch.

He left the office as quickly as he could. He had just gotten back on patrol when Dispatch called, "Clayton, call the Sheriff on his cell phone."

What the hell? Shit!

Clayton was still uneasy after his Mary Cole *Come to Jesus* meeting with the Sheriff. Had Cooper found out about the situation with Charlene?

How would he know about that? Charlene told me she didn't mention my name.

He had intended to stay out of Cooper's way until the Sheriff cooled down. His stomach tightened as he speed dialed the number.

Cooper picked up said. "Clayton, I know your personal weapon is a Berretta PX4. I need you to bring it in. Unless you have something on your plate at the moment, stop by your house now and drop it off at the office."

My Berretta? Really?

"What's the deal, Sheriff?" Clayton asked.

"Just do it," Cooper said and hung up.

Clayton did not like the sound of this. Why would he need to bring his gun in?

Forty-five minutes later, he dropped the pistol off.

221

"Is there a problem, Sheriff?"

Cooper looked tired and not in a good mood. "Look, Deputy," he replied with a flat-eyed stare. "The forensics are in, and the murder weapon was a PX4."

"And you think I might have done the killings?"

"Jesus H Christ, Clayton. Stop asking questions. Just give me your damn gun and get the hell out of here before I decide to consider you a suspect in these murders and throw you in jail."

Clayton wasn't sure how serious the Sheriff was, but he got out of the office as fast as he could.

xxx

When Anderson was gone, Cooper called Jim Priester at the FBI lab in Clarksburg.

"Jim," he said. "I have a couple of Berretta PX4s here. If I send them down this afternoon, could you expedite the rifling on them?"

"John, are you alright?" Priester asked.

"Don't ask," John said wearily. "It has been a hell of a day. I need to see if either weapon is a match for the bullets I sent you last week."

"Send them down, John. It won't take long. I'll do the tests myself. I have a couple of things on my plate, but can have the results to you first thing Monday morning."

"I owe you," John said and pushed the end button on his phone.

Cooper had one more call to make.

"Serdich, come by my office. I have a job for you."

CHAPTER 55

At ten o'clock Monday morning, Jim Priester called Cooper. "John, I hope you're doing better than the last time we talked."

"Yeah, I got away to the camp for the weekend. I needed it. What have you got?"

"I fired the weapons Friday afternoon and did the ballistic check on the slugs first thing this morning. Neither of them matches the murder weapon. Both are clean."

"Thanks, Jim," the Sheriff said. "Now I'm back to square one and have no idea who committed the murders." He disconnected the call.

Cooper sat for a long time looking at the evidence board. At first, he was convinced Ben killed Tony and Susan out of revenge, thinking Ben's PTSD could explain it. Tony's father's death was an odd coincidence, but when it turned out the old man was murdered, an added dimension came into the case making him unsure. In spite of this event, he needed to keep Ben in focus, so he set the old man's death to the side.

There were too many loose ends, and now with the weapon forensics in, he had no linking evidence and no suspect. Was there something he had missed?

He called Hank. "I'm releasing Ben this morning. The ballistics came back, and the slug didn't match Ben's weapon. But I guess you guys already knew that."

"Thanks for the call, John," Hank said. "I saw Ben a couple of times on the weekend. He has issues with confinement and was pretty uncomfortable. He was scared and pissed. I'm glad this is over."

"I also wanted you to know I did check Anderson's handgun and it was not a match either. Now I have two murders on my hands and have no damn idea what to do next," John said with resignation. "Come and get him if you want to."

"I'm on my way," Hank said. "Tell Ben I'll be there in thirty minutes. And by the way, John, thanks. Sorry for the way I behaved on Friday. We still good?"

"Yeah," John said. "We're still good."

xxx

When Hank arrived to get Ben, he asked Cooper if he had a little time.

"I do," he said. "Let's go to my office." The three men went into Cooper's office and shut the door. They sat down and glancing at each other at each other.

The Sheriff had questioned Ben but had not asked him who he thought might have committed the murders. Cooper started the conversation. "So, what do you want to talk about?"

Ben began, "John, Hank and I have a theory about the killings. We believe that it was all about Tony Cole."

Hank and Ben told Cooper they believed the murders of Tony and his father Gus were part of some kind of Mafia vendetta. At first, they weren't sure how the two deaths might be connected, but in their minds,

224

they were not a coincidence.

Hank said it was Gus's sister-in-law, Ann Stout, who initially had provided possible clues to this being more than three unconnected murders. Ann hadn't made any of the connections, but had helped connect the dots for them.

"This, of course, is just speculation," Hank said. "It probably doesn't help you solve the murders, but it does make sense."

"What about Susan? Any thoughts on how she fits in?" Cooper asked.

"We think Susan was in the wrong place at the wrong time," Ben said, shuffling his feet, looking down and growing silent.

Hank saw Cooper take a breath, stand up and pull Ben to his feet. He put his huge arms around his old friend and said, "I am really sorry about Susan's death, Ben. It was horrible. She didn't deserve this, and neither did you. As frustrating as this has been for me, if I had been in your shoes, I would have done the same damn thing."

xxx

That night, John Cooper met his father at their Colfax camp on the river. In the dark, John told him about the events and everything he knew.

"It sounds like it was touch and go with Ben," his dad said. "Like I said before, I've never had any experience with PTSD."

"Yeah," John replied, feeling the comfort of his father's presence and the warm night air. "I was pretty hard on him. If he'd lost it, things could have gotten real bad in a hurry. Thank God, they didn't. It was surreal. I think I was lucky."

"Your instincts were good, son. I'm glad you followed them."

"Hank was no picnic either. That guy's loyalty to Ben was palpable. Having him blow up right after dealing with Ben was almost too much," John said.

They sat and let the night air, the sound of the river and the chorus of crickets flood their senses.

John broke the silence, "In the end, I'm glad we were able to clear him. I also have to say, if it wasn't for Hank coming home and getting involved, things might have turned out real different. I got a feel for the kind of team those boys must have been."

"I've got some cleaning up to do with Clayton Anderson," he continued, "but he'll be okay. He was damned embarrassed about the Mary Cole thing. He said he was going to wait awhile and maybe give her a call."

"You know, son, Hank and Ben might have been right. It's not beyond the realm of possibility the murders were part of a mob contract that had been open for a long time. If that's the case, I doubt you will ever find the killer."

"You may be right, Dad," John said. "The problem is, now I have no idea what to do next."

They talked a little while longer before calling it a night. As they were getting in their cars, John said, "By the way, I just want you to know how helpful your advice was to share the evidence with Hank."

As Cooper drove home, he wondered to himself. *Will anyone ever pay?*

EPILOGUE

It was three o'clock on a Sunday morning, a month after the murders in Fairmont. The car pulled through the parking lot and parked at the back of H&S Heating and Cooling in Kennett Square, Pennsylvania. Two figures got out, removed some knapsacks from the trunk and slipped into the west branch of Red Clay Creek, behind the dumpsters at the back of the building.

Within an hour, they had made their way to the Northwestern corner of Giuseppe Asterino's horse farm, and went to work. Before the gradual shift from darkness to light took place, Ben and Hank had built an invisible nest, in a tree line three hundred fifty meters from the back of Asterino's mansion.

Scott Hardesty had done a little more digging. His sources confirmed Asterino, current head of the Philadelphia crime family, had contracted Delaney for the murders of Gus and Tony Cole. His sources also indicated Delaney would be at the Asterino estate on the weekend.

Mark Delaney had earned the trust of the Philadelphia Mafia. He succeeded where many others had failed since the murder of mob boss John Avena decades before. He had a reputation for getting his assignments done no matter what. This was no exception. He prided himself on finding the targets and taking them out. There was nobody better at contract killing than him, and he knew it.

Asterino was pleased, because the longstanding contract had been closed under his watch. He had invited Delaney to the farm to discuss a delicate matter regarding the removal of a Mafia leader residing in Florida.

Ben and Hank lay motionless in the nest through the day. Late in the afternoon with the sun at their backs they saw movement in the house.

Lying there, Ben's mind drifted to Susan. No one, not even Hank, would ever understand what had drawn him to her. He didn't even know. It was like breath, each exhale required the next inhale for life to continue. She was like that to him – like breath. He always believed someday he would understand her and feel that she was entirely his. Now she was gone, stolen before he could unwind the mystery that she had represented.

Asterino took Delaney out to the pool deck in the back yard. They sat in chairs at an umbrella-covered table.

"Targets," Hank whispered to Ben.

"Targets acquired," Ben quietly replied.

Ben sighted Susan's killer in his scope.

"Range three hundred fifty meters," Hank said, continuing to focus on Delaney.

Hank remembered their first assignment in Iraq, when they had missed the *RAG*. Ironically, the distance was exactly the same for this final mission. All the years they spent together on the hunt, all the killings they had done in the service of their country, were behind them now. They made up for that first miss, and became one of America's elite sniper teams. One thing was certain as they lay on the ground on the edge of a Mafia Don's horse farm in Pennsylvania – they wouldn't miss today.

"Roger and ready," Ben calmly replied.

Focused like predators to the prey, Hank said, "Take the shot."

ABOUT THE AUTHOR

Tom Edwards has traveled extensively in the United States, Asia and Europe. His formative years were spent in Fairmont, West Virginia nestled along the banks of the Monongahela River in the Appalachian Mountains. It is the people from this part of the country and the hills in which they live that shaped much of the way he thinks. Like others before him, mentors and helpers emerged at just the right time in his life to guide and lead him. He is a veteran of the Vietnam war, an experience that provided him with insight and respect for those that protect us from unseen dangers.

He lives with Molly his wife, Hannah and Leah his cats all of whom have managed to slip through life with grace.

Made in the USA
Columbia, SC
16 November 2017